Volume **13** THE GOLDEN BOOK ENCYCLOPEDIA

New Brunswick to Ozark Mountains

new-oz

An exciting, up-to-date encyclopedia
in 20 fact-filled, entertaining volumes

Especially designed as
a first encyclopedia for
today's grade-school children

More than 2,500 full-color
photographs and illustrations

GOLDEN ®

From the Publishers of Golden® Books

Western Publishing Company, Inc.
Racine, Wisconsin 53404

ILLUSTRATION CREDITS
(t=top, b=bottom, c=center, l=left, r=right)

1 l, Lloyd P. Birmingham; 1 r, John Rice/Joseph, Mindlin & Mulvey Inc.; 3 cr, Arthur Sirdofsky; 3 br, David Lindroth Inc.; 5 bl, David Lindroth Inc.; 5 br, Dan Guravich/Photo Researchers; 7 tl, Marilyn Bass; 7 br, Porterfield- Chickering/Photo Researchers; 9 tl, Marilyn Bass; 9 cr, Courtesy of New Jersey Travel and Tourism; 11 tr, Marilyn Bass; 11 bl, Georg Gerster/Photo Researchers; 12, montage by Laurie Bender/Copyright 1988 *USA Today*, excerpted with permission (photo left, Brian Hamill/Photoreporters; photo center, Richard Derk); 13, Gary Lippincott/Publishers' Graphics; 14 tr and 15 tl, Marilyn Bass; 15 tr, © Joe Viesti; 16 bl, H.B. Jenssen; 16 br, © Joe Viesti; 17, David Lindroth Inc.; 18 bl, Earl Dibble/Photo Researchers; 19, Tom Hollyman/Photo Researchers; 20, David Lindroth Inc.; 21, Marc and Evelyne Bernheim/Woodfin Camp; 22 both, Culver Pictures; 24 b, Magnum; 25, M. Philippot/Sygma; 26 bl, T. Campion/Sygma; 26 br, J.-P. Laffont/Sygma; 27, Victor Englebert/Photo Researchers; 28, David Lindroth Inc.; 29 tl, Earl Roberge/Photo Researchers; 29 cl, Watriss-Baldwin/Woodfin Camp; 29 tr, David Lindroth Inc.; 31 t, David Lindroth Inc.; 31 bl, Jim Anderson/Woodfin Camp; 32 bl, Lee Foster/Bruce Coleman Inc.; 32 br, James Hanley/Photo Researchers; 33, Craig Aurness/Woodfin Camp; 34 tr, Marilyn Bass; 35 cl, North Carolina Department of Commerce; 37 tr, Marilyn Bass; 37 bl, Norris Taylor/Photo Researchers; 38, Ned Haines/Photo Researchers; 41 b, The Granger Collection; 41 inset, David Lindroth Inc.; 42 bl, Canadian Department of Regional Industrial Expansion; 42 br and 43 tr, David Lindroth Inc.; 43 br, Ned Haines/Photo Researchers; 45 t, Tom Powers/Joseph, Mindlin & Mulvey Inc.; 45 cl, Dan McCoy/Rainbow; 45 br, Official U.S. Navy Photograph; 46 br, Brad Hamann; 46 t, U.S. Department of Energy; 46 inset and br, Brad Hamann; 47, David Lindroth Inc.; 48 tl, Turi MacCombie/Evelyne Johnson Associates; 49, Dennis O'Brien/Joseph, Mindlin & Mulvey Inc.; 51 bl, Lloyd P. Birmingham; 51 br, John Elk III/Bruce Coleman Inc.; 52 and 53 r, Tanya Rebelo/Joseph, Mindlin & Mulvey Inc.; 53 tl, Gordon E. Smith/Photo Researchers; 54, Walter Gaffney- Kessell/Publishers' Graphics; 55 bl, Culver Pictures; 56, Francois Gohier/Photo Researchers; 57, David Lindroth Inc.; 58–59 t, Van Bucher/Photo Researchers; 59 inset, Rodney Catanach/Woods Hole Oceanographic Institution; 60, David Lindroth Inc.; 61, Bill Curtsinger/Photo Researchers; 62–63 b, Dennis O'Brien/Joseph, Mindlin & Mulvey Inc.; 63 tl, P.M. David/Photo Researchers; 63 tr, Tom McHugh/ Photo Researchers; 64 b, Shirley/Richards/Photo Researchers; 64 inset, Eric Grave/Photo Researchers; 65 t, E.D. Robinson/Tom Stack & Associates; 65 inset, Peter David/Photo Researchers; 67 tr, Jack Kraczyk/Convention and Visitors' Bureau of Cleveland; 67 bl, Marilyn Bass; 68, David Lindroth Inc.; 69 br, American Petroleum Institute; 69 inset, Junebug Clark/Photo Researchers; 70, Brad Hamann; 71 tl, Don Girvin/Bruce Coleman Inc.; 71 b, Texaco Inc./American Petroleum Institute; 72, Tom Powers/Joseph, Mindlin & Mulvey Inc.; 73 tl, B.J. Nixon/Tenneco, Inc./American Petroleum Institute; 73 br, Georgia O'Keeffe, *The Mountain, New Mexico,* 1931, oil on canvas, 30 x 36 inches, Collection of Whitney Museum of American Art, Purchase, 32.14; 75 bl, © Joe Viesti; 75 rc, Marilyn Bass; 77 t, Focus on Sports; 77 inset, David Lindroth Inc.; 78–79 all, Focus on Sports; 80 bl, David Lindroth Inc.; 80 br, Candian Department of Regional Industrial Expansion; 82, Rebecca Lesher/Martha Swope Associates; 84, Steve Maslowski/Photo Researchers; 85, © 1987 by Marianne Barcellona, courtesy The New York Philharmonic Orchestra, Zubin Mehta--Music Director, Itzhak Perlman-- violin soloist; 86–87, Marie DeJohn/Publishers' Graphics; 89 tl, Marilyn Bass; 89 bl, William H. Mullins/Photo Researchers; 90 b, Historical Pictures Service, Chicago; 90 inset, David Lindroth Inc.; 91, Lloyd P. Birmingham; 92, M.P. Kahl/Photo Researchers; 93 tl, Jeff Foott/Bruce Coleman Inc.; 93 br, AP/Wide World; 94 all, John Rice/Joseph, Mindlin & Mulvey Inc.; 96 tl, Joy Spurr/Bruce Coleman Inc.; 96 b, Kent and Donna Dannen/Photo Researchers; 96 inset, David Lindroth Inc.

COVER CREDITS
Center: John Rice/Joseph, Mindlin & Mulvey Inc. Clockwise from top: Francois Gohier/Photo Researchers; Steve Maslowski/Photo Researchers; B.J. Nixon/Tenneco, Inc./American Petroleum Institute; E.D. Robinson/Tom Stack & Associates; Focus on Sports; David Lindroth Inc.

Library of Congress Catalog Card Number: 87-82741
ISBN: 0-307-70113-1

ABCDEFGHIJK

continued

New Brunswick

Capital: Fredericton
Area: 28,360 square miles (73,452 square kilometers) (8th-largest province)
Population (1981): 696,403 (1985): about 717,200 (8th-largest province)
Became a province: July 1, 1867 (one of four original provinces)

New Brunswick is the second largest of Canada's four Atlantic Provinces—Nova Scotia, Newfoundland, New Brunswick, and Prince Edward Island. Quebec Province lies to the north of New Brunswick. The Bay of Fundy lies to the south. The Gulf of St. Lawrence is to the east. New Brunswick's western border is shared with Maine.

Land New Brunswick is well known for its natural beauty. Thick forests cover much of its land. Rivers flow down hills and through valleys on their way to the sea. One famous river, the St. John, sometimes flows backward, up a waterfall!

The St. John River empties into the Bay of Fundy. The *tides* of the bay—among the highest in the world—are what makes the river flow backward. Tides are the rising and falling of ocean water twice a day. At low tide, the waters in the Bay of Fundy flow out toward the Atlantic Ocean. At high tide, the ocean water rushes back into the bay. The

water may be up to 50 feet (15 meters) deeper at high tide than at low tide. High tide is so strong that it pushes the water of the St. John River back up over a series of rocky ledges. This creates what are known as the Reversing Falls.

Rolling hills cover northern and western New Brunswick. The eastern and central parts of the province are lowlands. Forests blanket almost nine-tenths of New Brunswick. Their lumber was used for shipbuilding during the 1800s. Today, balsam firs and spruce provide wood for many other uses, including the manufacture of paper and paper products. The province also exports Christmas trees to the United States.

Some boats in this New Brunswick harbor use wooden traps to catch lobsters.

New Brunswick's east coast is known for its scenic fishing villages. Fishing is a major industry in New Brunswick and in the other Atlantic Provinces. Inshore fishermen keep their small boats within 15 miles (24 kilometers) of the coast. They catch cod, scallops, herring, salmon, and lobster. Offshore fishermen sail larger boats called *trawlers* 50 miles (80 kilometers) or more off the coast. There, they fish for cod, haddock, flounder, and herring.

Farming is not a major activity in New Brunswick because much of the soil is rocky and not very fertile. Potatoes are grown in the St. John River Valley, and dairy farms are scattered throughout the province. Large deposits of lead, copper, zinc, and silver were discovered in New Brunswick about 40 years ago.

History The Micmac and the Malecite Indians lived in what is now New Brunswick before the Europeans arrived. New Brunswick was settled by the French during the 1600s. They set up many colonies along the Atlantic coast from Quebec to Maine. They named this area Acadia.

England gained control of Acadia in 1713. The Acadians remained loyal to France, however, and caused trouble for the British. Finally in 1755, the British told the Acadians they had to leave. Many of them journeyed far to the south. They went down the Mississippi River and settled in Louisiana. But some hid in the forests of New Brunswick. Eventually, they came out of hiding and were joined by others, who had returned from the United States.

During the 1760s, many British farmers moved to New Brunswick. They were given land that had belonged to the Acadians. When the American Revolutionary War broke out, thousands of American colonists who were loyal to England moved to New Brunswick and other Canadian settlements. These people, called the United Empire Loyalists, had been among the wealthiest American colonists, and they became a powerful group in Canada.

New Brunswick was part of Nova Scotia until 1784, when it became a separate province. New Brunswick joined with Ontario, Quebec, and Nova Scotia to form the Dominion of Canada in 1867.

People A little more than half of the people in New Brunswick are of British descent. About a third are descended from the French. There are also more than 5,000 Indians in New Brunswick.

Over half of the people live in towns and cities. Saint John is New Brunswick's largest city. It is located at the end of the Canadian Pacific Railway, and its busy port remains free of ice all year long. About one-fifth of the province's people live in or around Saint John.

Fredericton is the capital of New Brunswick. It is a small city about 60 miles (97 kilometers) from the city of Saint John. Fredericton's factories make boots, shoes, canoes, and other products. It is also the home of the University of New Brunswick.

Newfoundland

Capital: St. John's
Area: 156,650 square miles (405,724 square kilometers) (7th-largest province)
Population (1981): 567,681 (1985): about 578,900 (9th-largest province)
Became a province: March 31, 1949 (10th and newest province)

Newfoundland is the newest Canadian province and one of the oldest settled areas in North America. The province includes the island of Newfoundland, in the Atlantic Ocean, and Labrador, just across the Strait of Belle Isle on Canada's mainland. Newfoundland is one of Canada's four Atlantic Provinces. New Brunswick, Nova Scotia, and Prince Edward Island are the other three.

Land Labrador lies between the Atlantic Ocean and the province of Quebec. The land is rocky and cold, and covered with forests. Labrador is rich in natural resources. More than a third of all the iron ore in Canada comes from mines in Labrador. The forests provide timber, wood pulp, and paper. Labrador also has one of the largest hydroelectric plants in North America. Oil and natural gas were discovered off the coast of Labrador in 1976.

The island of Newfoundland has a rugged coast indented with many bays. The island has forests, lakes, bogs, and *barrens*—stony areas where only low-growing trees, moss, and some flowering plants can survive.

People Vikings from Iceland and Greenland came to Newfoundland around the year 1000 and set up summer fishing camps. In the late 1400s, European fishermen began coming to Newfoundland again. The island was under British control from 1583 until 1949, when it became a province of Canada.

Most of Newfoundland's people live in towns and villages along the jagged coast, where the winters are a bit warmer. Fishing is still a way of life for many. There are more fishermen in Newfoundland than in any other Canadian province. The capital city, St. John's, is home port for many of them. Cod, flounder, and sole are among the kinds of fish that are brought back and processed in the city's factories. More than a quarter of the people in the province live in and around St. John's.

Corner Brook, in western Newfoundland, is the only other large town in the province. It was built up around one of the world's largest pulp and paper mills. Many of Newfoundland's other settlements have fewer that 1,000 people.

The province has a university, more than 100 libraries, several museums, and one of Canada's finest international airports.

Coastal fishermen in Newfoundland work together to haul in a cod trap.

Map

Cape Chidley

Labrador Sea

QUEBEC

N E W F O U N D L A N D

Labrador

Smallwood Reservoir

Lobstick Lake

Lake Melville

Battle Harbour

QUEBEC

ATLANTIC OCEAN

Gulf of St. Lawrence

TERRA NOVA NATIONAL PARK

Corner Brook

Gander

Stephenville

Newfoundland

St. John's ★

Cabot Strait

Placentia Bay

Feet above sea level

2,000
1,000
500
0
Below sea level

0   100   200   300 Miles

0   100   200   300 Kilometers

New Hampshire

Capital: Concord
Area: 9,279 square miles (24,033 square kilometers) (44th-largest state)
Population (1980): 920,610 (1985): about 998,000 (41st-largest state)
Became a state: June 21, 1788 (9th state)

New Hampshire is a state in the northeastern United States. It was one of the original thirteen colonies, and the first to have its own constitution and declare independence from England. In 1945, the state adopted as its motto a saying from the American Revolution—"Live Free or Die."

New Hampshire is one of six states that make up the region called New England. The Canadian province of Quebec lies to the north of New Hampshire. Massachusetts is to the south. Maine and 18 miles (29 kilometers) of Atlantic coastline are to the east. Vermont is to the west.

Land Almost all of New Hampshire is hilly or mountainous. Many rivers and streams rise in the hills, and there are more than 1,000 lakes in the state. Water from the largest lake, Lake Winnipesaukee, eventually flows into the Merrimack River. Other major rivers include the Connecticut, Androscoggin, and Piscataqua.

Mount Washington, in New Hampshire's White Mountains, is the highest point in the northeastern United States. It rises 6,288 feet (1,917 meters) above sea level. It is one of 47 peaks in the White Mountains that are more than 4,000 feet (1,219 meters) high. Anyone who climbs all 47 peaks can join the Four Thousand Footer Club. The club has more than 2,000 members, including a six-year-old boy, a man in his seventies—and even a collie!

Most of New Hampshire is covered with forests. Crops do not grow well in the sandy, stony soil. Agriculture is a major activity only in the valley of the Connecticut River, along New Hampshire's western border.

Summers are pleasantly cool in New Hampshire. Winters are cold and snowy. New Hampshire can be windy, too. The strongest wind ever recorded anywhere in the world—231 miles (372 kilometers) per hour—hit Mount Washington in 1934.

New Hampshire's nickname is the "Granite State." At one time, granite was a widely used building material. In the early 1900s, New Hampshire led the nation in the quarrying of granite. Now, the state mines mostly sand and gravel. These materials are used in building roads.

History Around the year 1000, Vikings explored the Atlantic coast of New Hampshire. They may have lived there for two or three winters. English explorers and settlers began to arrive in the early 1620s. Settlement started in the southeastern part of the state, near what is now the city of Portsmouth. Pioneers moved gradually inland, but their progress was slowed by Indians.

At times in its history, New Hampshire was part of the colony of Massachusetts. At other times, it was a separate province. In January 1776, it set up a government independent of England.

During the 1800s, manufacturing developed. The state had a large number of people willing to work, and good supplies of waterpower and raw materials, such as wood. Its manufactured goods were easily sent by train or ship to cities along the eastern coast of the United States.

Textiles used to be the state's leading product. In fact, more cotton cloth used to be woven in the city of Manchester than in any other city in the world. Manchester is still the state's leading industrial city, even though the cotton mills have moved to the southern United States.

New Hampshire also manufactures shoes and other leather products, machinery, wood

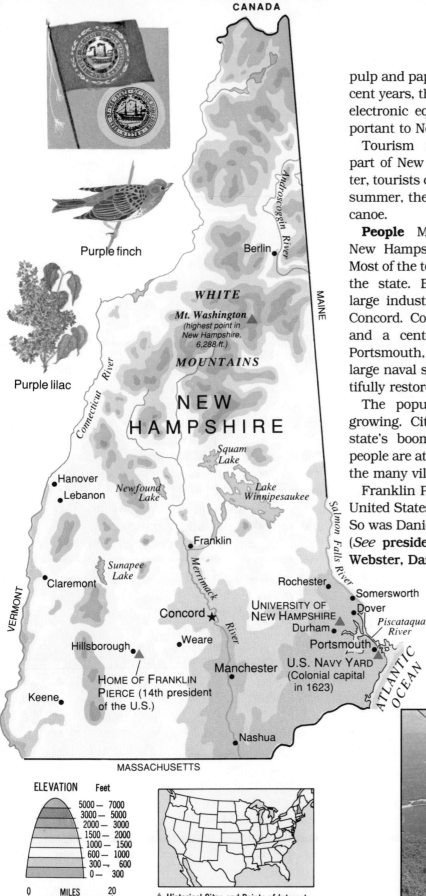

Purple finch

Purple lilac

CANADA

Androscoggin River

Berlin

MAINE

WHITE

Mt. Washington
(highest point in
New Hampshire,
6,288 ft.)

MOUNTAINS

NEW
HAMPSHIRE

Connecticut River

*Squam
Lake*

*Lake
Winnipesaukee*

Hanover
Lebanon

*Newfound
Lake*

Franklin

Salmon Falls River

Sunapee
Lake

Claremont

Merrimack

Rochester

Somersworth

VERMONT

Concord ★

UNIVERSITY OF
NEW HAMPSHIRE

Dover

*Piscataqua
River*

Durham

Weare

River

Portsmouth

Hillsborough ▲

HOME OF FRANKLIN
PIERCE (14th president
of the U.S.)

Manchester

U.S. NAVY YARD
(Colonial capital
in 1623)

Keene

*ATLANTIC
OCEAN*

Nashua

MASSACHUSETTS

ELEVATION   Feet

5000 — 7000
3000 — 5000
2000 — 3000
1500 — 2000
1000 — 1500
600 — 1000
300 — 600
0 — 300

0   MILES   20

▲ Historical Sites and Points of Interest

pulp and paper products, and plastics. In recent years, the manufacture of electrical and electronic equipment has become very important to New Hampshire's economy.

Tourism is the second-most-important part of New Hampshire's economy. In winter, tourists come to ski in the mountains. In summer, they come to hike, camp, fish, and canoe.

People More than half of the people in New Hampshire live in cities and towns. Most of the towns are in the southern part of the state. Besides Manchester, there are large industrial complexes in Nashua and Concord. Concord is also the state capital and a center for publishing magazines. Portsmouth, on the Atlantic coast, has a large naval shipyard and a number of beautifully restored colonial buildings.

The population of New Hampshire is growing. City people are attracted to the state's booming industrial centers. Other people are attracted to the peace and quiet of the many villages tucked away in the hills.

Franklin Pierce, the 14th president of the United States, was a New Hampshire native. So was Daniel Webster, the great statesman. (*See* **presidents of the United States** and **Webster, Daniel.**)

A tram takes visitors to the top of Cannon Mountain, where they can view the beautiful countryside around them.

New Jersey

Capital: Trenton

Area: 7,787 square miles
(20,168 square kilometers)
(46th-largest state)

Population (1980): 7,365,011
(1985): about 7,562,000
(9th-largest state)

Became a state: December 18, 1787
(3rd state)

New Jersey is a state in the northeastern United States. It is a small state with a large population. In fact, there are more people per square mile in New Jersey than in any other state!

New Jersey is bordered on the north by New York, and on the south by Delaware Bay. On the east, it is bordered by the Hudson River and the Atlantic Ocean. Pennsylvania is to the west. The Delaware River forms the western and southern boundaries.

Land The northwestern third of New Jersey is mountainous. The rest of the land is low and either flat or gently rolling. Forests cover large areas in the southern part of the state. Summers are warm and humid, and winters are cold.

There are different kinds of soils in New Jersey. In the mountains, the soil is stony. In the center of the state, it is fertile. Along the coast, it is sandy and not very rich.

Water has been very important to New Jersey's development. Its bays and coastal rivers have good harbors for oceangoing ships. Its rivers provide transportation and hydroelectric power. Modern chemical industries use a great deal of water, so they line the banks of the Passaic and Raritan rivers, in northern New Jersey. The Atlantic coast—called the Jersey Shore—attracts tourists to its cities and beach towns. New Jersey's many beautiful lakes are also popular with tourists.

History The first European to see New Jersey was probably Giovanni da Verrazano, an Italian navigator. He explored the Atlantic coast in 1524. In 1609, Henry Hudson explored the river that later was named after him. Soon afterward, Dutch and Swedish settlers arrived. The early colonists were at peace with the friendly Delaware Indians living in the area.

The British took over all of the Dutch lands in America in 1664. After that, British settlers began to arrive in New Jersey. The colony was divided in two. West Jersey was the first Quaker colony in America. It traded with Philadelphia, in Pennsylvania. (*See* Quakers.)

East Jersey was settled mainly by Puritans. It had links with New York City. England united the two Jerseys in 1702.

Settlers from Europe arrived in New Jersey all during the 1600s and 1700s. In 1758, the first Indian reservation in the United States was established at Indian Mills.

New Jersey played a major role in the American Revolution. The colony lay between two important cities—New York City and Philadelphia—and many battles were fought on New Jersey soil. Princeton, New Jersey, served as the nation's capital from June to November 1783.

New Jersey had many things that enabled industry to develop early. It had waterpower and a growing population. Goods could be shipped easily by river or ocean to nearby cities, where they could be sold. In colonial times, New Jersey was known for its glass, leather, iron, and lumber products.

After the colonies became independent from England, industry grew rapidly in New Jersey. In 1791, Alexander Hamilton helped to found Paterson, the first planned industrial town in the United States.

People New Jersey is still a leading industrial state. Most workers are involved in manufacturing. There are factories throughout the state, but most of them are near Newark, the largest city. New Jersey's factories lead the nation in the production of

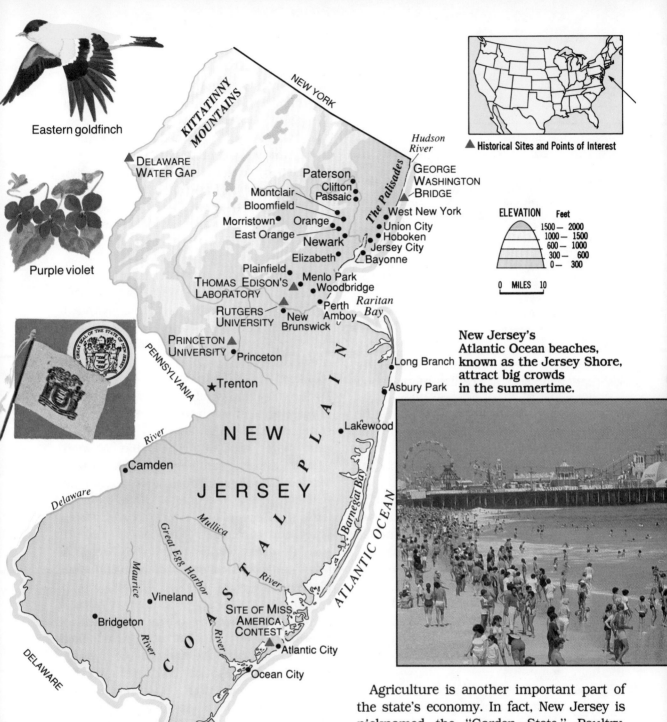

Eastern goldfinch

Purple violet

KITTATINNY MOUNTAINS

NEW YORK

Hudson River

DELAWARE WATER GAP

Paterson
Clifton
Montclair Passaic
Bloomfield
Morristown Orange
East Orange
Newark
Elizabeth

The Palisades

GEORGE WASHINGTON BRIDGE

West New York
Union City
Hoboken
Jersey City
Bayonne

▲ Historical Sites and Points of Interest

ELEVATION   Feet

1500 — 2000
1000 — 1500
600 — 1000
300 — 600
0 — 300

0   MILES   10

Plainfield
THOMAS EDISON'S LABORATORY
Menlo Park
Woodbridge
Perth Amboy
RUTGERS UNIVERSITY
New Brunswick

Raritan Bay

PRINCETON UNIVERSITY
Princeton

PENNSYLVANIA

★ Trenton

Long Branch
Asbury Park

New Jersey's Atlantic Ocean beaches, known as the Jersey Shore, attract big crowds in the summertime.

N E W

Lakewood

River

J E R S E Y

Camden

Delaware

Mullica

Great Egg Harbor

Maurice

Vineland

River

Bridgeton

River

River

C O A S T A L   P L A I N

Barnegat Bay

ATLANTIC OCEAN

SITE OF MISS AMERICA CONTEST
Atlantic City

Ocean City

DELAWARE

Delaware Bay

Cape May

Agriculture is another important part of the state's economy. In fact, New Jersey is nicknamed the "Garden State." Poultry, fruit, vegetable, and dairy farming are the major activities. Corn, wheat, oats, soybeans, and hay are the leading crops.

Almost all New Jerseyans live in cities. Most of the large cities are clustered along the highway between Philadelphia and New York City. These include Newark, Jersey City, Camden, Elizabeth, and Trenton, the state capital. Atlantic City, a beach resort, is on the Jersey Shore.

chemicals and chemical products—such as perfume, plastics, building materials, vitamins, and vaccines. New Jersey is also a leading producer of clothing, electrical and electronic goods, aircraft, automobiles, and railroad equipment.

New Mexico

Capital: Santa Fe
Area: 121,593 square miles (314,926 square kilometers) (5th-largest state)
Population (1980): 1,303,302 (1985): about 1,450,000 (37th-largest state)
Became a state: January 6, 1912 (47th state)

New Mexico is a state in the southwestern United States. Its beautiful deserts, mountains, canyons, and clear air have earned it the nickname "Land of Enchantment."

New Mexico is bordered by Colorado to the north, Arizona to the west, Mexico to the south, and Texas to the south and east. New Mexico meets Oklahoma in the northeast corner of the state.

Land The eastern third of New Mexico is flat, except for an occasional mountain, canyon, or *mesa*—flat-topped hill. Most of the rest of the state is hilly or mountainous. The Rocky Mountains reach into northern New Mexico. (*See* **Rocky Mountains.**)

Different kinds of plants grow in New Mexico's various regions. Sagebrush and cacti dot the desert areas. The plains are covered with grasses. Evergreen trees grow in the high mountains.

The climate is dry and mild. Daytime temperatures can be hot, but it is always cool at night. In the mountains, there is a lot of snow in winter. The rest of the state receives only about 10 inches (25 centimeters) of rain a year. For this reason, water is precious. Reservoirs have been built to store water for drinking and for irrigating farmland.

New Mexico's land is rich in petroleum, potash, copper, and natural gas. The most important mineral is uranium. Almost three-quarters of the uranium in the United States is found in New Mexico.

The largest gypsum desert in the world is in White Sands National Monument. Gypsum is a powdery white mineral—hydrous calcium sulfate. Gypsum deserts are made up of shifting, gleaming white dunes.

Carlsbad Caverns National Park is in New Mexico. Carlsbad Caverns form the world's largest system of caves. One of the caverns is the largest in the world. It measures 1,500 by 300 feet (457 by 91 meters), and is 300 feet (91 meters) high.

History People have lived in the area since prehistoric times. Spear points made by Sandia man 10,000 to 12,000 years ago have been found in mountain caves. Later peoples built cities of hundreds and sometimes thousands of joined rooms. They established trade routes that reached the Pacific coast and what is now Mexico. Ruins of these ancient civilizations are protected in state and national parks.

In more recent times, Pueblo, Navaho, Apache, and Ute Indians have lived in New Mexico. One Pueblo tribe, the Taos Indians, still live in cliff dwellings. Another Pueblo tribe, the Zuni, make beautiful jewelry from silver and turquoise. The Navaho, too, are skillful silver workers and also weavers. Many museums collect their beautiful wool blankets and rugs.

Early Spanish explorers had heard tales of seven very rich cities north of Mexico. A Spanish priest named Marcos de Niza looked for them in 1539 and claimed the area for Spain. In 1540, Francisco Vásquez de Coronado set out in search of seven cities. Instead, he found Indian pueblos built of adobe, stone, and wood. In 1610, the territorial capital was established at Santa Fe. Santa Fe is still the capital of New Mexico and the oldest capital city in the nation.

New Mexico became a U.S. territory in 1850, after the Mexican War. It became a state in 1912. (*See* **Mexican War.**)

Cattle ranching developed in the 1870s, and sheep ranching shortly afterward. Agriculture became more widespread after the Elephant Butte Dam was completed in 1916.

UTAH • COLORADO • OKLAHOMA

Farmington
San Juan River
AZTEC RUINS
NATIONAL MONUMENT
Navajo Reservoir
Raton

NAVAJO INDIAN
RESERVATION
(largest in the U.S.)

Taos

Los Alamos
Santa Fe
Las Vegas

Gallup
SITE OF ANNUAL CEREMONIAL
DANCES OF THE NAVAJOS,
APACHES, AND PUEBLOS

OLDEST CITY
IN THE WEST

Conchas
Lake

Tucumcari

Grants

Albuquerque
UNIVERSITY OF
NEW MEXICO

ACOMA PUEBLO (believed
to be the oldest inhabited
pueblo in the U.S.)

ENCHANTED
MESA

Belen

GRAVE OF
BILLY THE KID

Fort Sumner

Clovis

N E W   M E X I C O
Portales

Socorro

Rio Grande

Roswell

Pecos River

Truth or
Consequences

Silver City

Alamogordo
Artesia
Lovington

Hobbs

WHITE SANDS
MISSILE RANGE
WHITE SANDS
NATIONAL
MONUMENT

Carlsbad

Las Cruces

Deming

MEXICO

ARIZONA • TEXAS

▲ Historical Sites and Points of Interest

Roadrunner

Yucca blossom

ELEVATION   Feet
Over 10000
7000 — 10000
5000 — 7000
3000 — 5000
2000 — 3000

0   MILES   40

Flat-topped hills called *mesas* appear in many parts of New Mexico.

Since World War II, New Mexico has been a center for energy and weapons research. The first atomic bomb was exploded in 1945 near Alamogordo.

People New Mexico has a small population. About a third of its people are descendants of settlers who came from Spain or Mexico in colonial times. Most of these people live in cities or on farms along the Rio Grande—a river that flows south through the middle of the state. (*See* **Rio Grande.**)

Almost three-quarters of the people live in cities or towns. The largest is Albuquerque—a manufacturing, educational, and tourist center in north-central New Mexico.

The U.S. government is the largest employer in New Mexico. Service industries—including shops and restaurants supported by New Mexico's tourist industry—are the second-largest source of income. Mining and farming are also important.

11

A newspaper gives readers news, weather, and sports reports. It gives movie and television schedules and carries advertisements.

newspaper

Each day, a newspaper is published in your city, or in a city nearby. Someone may deliver it to your house, or you may buy it from a machine, newsstand, or store.

A newspaper has an amazing amount of information in it. It has news stories from many parts of the world. It reports the scores of yesterday's sporting events. It provides weather information and forecasts. It also includes special features—such as comic strips, crossword puzzles, and articles about food, home decorating, and entertainment.

Newspapers also carry advertisements. People who want a new job or a used car look in the *classified advertising.* Others look for entertainment ads. They tell what movies are playing and what programs are on television. People also use newspaper ads to learn about special sales in stores. Advertising is important to a newspaper. The paper gets most of its money from people and businesses who pay to advertise.

How does a newspaper put together all this material every day? A large newspaper may have hundreds of workers helping to put the paper together. Many papers publish every day, year-round, so work on a newspaper never stops.

News comes from reporters. They gather facts, interview people, and write the stories. Sometimes they send their stories in by phone or on a teletype machine. Editors decide how much room to give different stories. They also check them to be sure that they are clear and correct.

At the same time, other workers are preparing the advertisements. Others are setting news and ads in type and fitting the type and pictures on each page. Still others are getting printing presses ready to print thousands of copies of the paper.

Finally, the *deadline* comes. After this time, no new material can be put in that day's paper. Workers make a *plate* of each page and attach the plates to high-speed printing presses. Then the presses begin to run. Paper from giant rolls is fed into them. The paper is printed on both sides, cut into newspaper-size sheets, assembled, and folded. A single press can print thousands of papers an hour. (*See* **printing**.)

When the newspapers come off the press, there are trucks ready to carry bundles of them to newspaper carriers, newsstands, and stores. Everyone for miles around can buy the newspaper that day. Even as the papers are being delivered, other workers are planning tomorrow's paper.

newt, *see* salamanders and newts

Newton, Sir Isaac

Sir Isaac Newton was an English scientist and one of the world's greatest thinkers. His ideas helped to explain light, color, motion, gravity, and mathematics.

Newton was born on Christmas Day in 1642. After a very unhappy childhood, he attended Cambridge University. He was already developing his mathematical ideas. Later, his methods grew into a branch of mathematics called *calculus.*

Newton claimed that he got his ideas about gravity from seeing an apple fall at his mother's farm. He decided that the same force that pulled the apple to Earth must also pull the moon. Newton used this idea—that there are gravitational forces between all objects—to explain why the planets orbit the sun, and why the moon orbits the earth.

Sir Isaac Newton studied how gravity works on Earth, then applied what he learned to the moon, the planets, and the sun.

Newton showed that white light is made up of all the colors of the rainbow. First he held a glass prism up to a beam of sunlight, letting the beam of light pass through it. The prism separated the light into all of its colors. Then he passed the colored beam through another prism to make white light again. Isaac Newton also made the first telescope that used mirrors instead of lenses. (*See* **telescope.**)

Newton wrote about his experiments and ideas. His most important book is the *Principia,* published in 1687. It describes his theory of gravity and three laws of motion. In *Opticks* (1704), Newton wrote about his experiments with light.

See also **gravity; light;** and **motion.**

New Year's Day

New Year's Day is the first day of the year. In most countries, this is January 1. The evening before, December 31, is called *New Year's Eve.*

New Year's Day is a holiday celebrated around the world. People gather together on New Year's Eve to say good-bye to the old year and welcome the new one. In the United States, millions of people watch New Year's Eve celebrations on television. Cities hold special events to mark the beginning of the new year. The most famous one takes place at Times Square in New York City.

For many, the new year is a time to make *resolutions*—promises—to improve themselves. Popular resolutions include going on a diet, exercising more, being kinder, and learning something new. Church services are often held on New Year's Eve and New Year's Day. Some people celebrate January 1 by visiting family and friends. Others enjoy watching parades and football games on television.

For many people, the new year is celebrated at a different time. The Chinese New Year begins sometime between January 21 and February 19. The Jewish New Year, *Rosh Hashanah,* is in autumn.

New York

Capital: Albany
Area: 49,108 square miles (127,190 square kilometers) (30th-largest state)
Population (1980): 17,558,165 (1985): about 17,783,000 (2nd-largest state)
Became a state: July 26, 1788 (11th state)

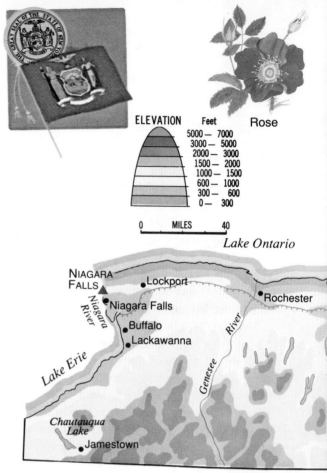

ELEVATION Feet Rose

5000 — 7000	
3000 — 5000	
2000 — 3000	
1500 — 2000	
1000 — 1500	
600 — 1000	
300 — 600	
0 — 300	

0   MILES   40

New York is a state in the northeastern United States. It is nicknamed the "Empire State" because George Washington is said to have remarked that New York could be the "seat of the empire"—a place from which the United States could be run.

New York is bordered on the north by Canada, on the south by New Jersey and Pennsylvania, and on the east by Vermont, Massachusetts, and Connecticut. Its southeastern corner opens on the Atlantic Ocean. New York's Long Island reaches 118 miles (190 kilometers) eastward from this corner along the coast of Connecticut.

Land New York's many rivers and lakes provide transportation, recreation, hydroelectric power, and drinking water. Lake Erie and Lake Ontario give the state a way to ship goods along the St. Lawrence Seaway. The Niagara River, between the two lakes, spills over magnificent falls. (*See* **Great Lakes; St. Lawrence River;** and **Niagara Falls.**)

The Hudson River flows south to New York Bay, a major port. Another important river, the Mohawk, flows from western New York into the Hudson just north of Albany, the state capital.

New York has fertile farmlands, sandy beaches, rolling hills, and mountains. The Adirondack Mountains lie in the northern part of the state. The Appalachian Plateau, which includes the Catskill Mountains, covers the southern half of the state. Lowlands

border Lake Champlain, Lake Ontario, Lake Erie, and the St. Lawrence River. The Hudson and Mohawk river valleys form a *Y* in east-central New York State.

History The first European to spot New York was probably Giovanni da Verrazano, an Italian. He explored the Atlantic coast in 1524. In 1609 Henry Hudson, an English navigator working for the Dutch, sailed up the river now named for him. (*See* **Hudson, Henry.**)

Dutch traders claimed the area Hudson explored, and named it New Netherland. In 1624, some Dutch families sailed up the Hudson River and established the colony's first European settlement, Fort Orange— later called Albany. Only a few colonists remained at Manhattan Island—now part of New York City. But more colonists from the Netherlands joined them. In 1626, the colony's governor, Peter Minuit, bought Manhattan Island from the Indians for $24

14

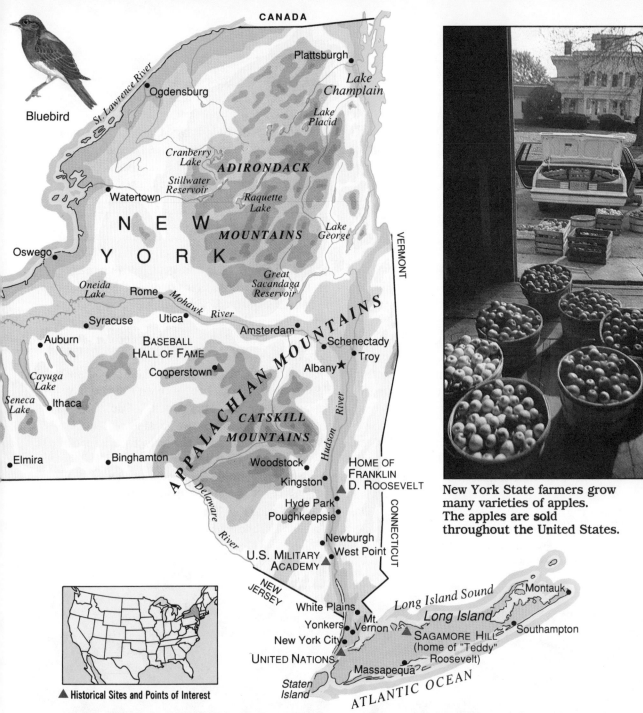

Bluebird

CANADA

Plattsburgh

Lake Champlain

Ogdensburg

Lake Placid

St. Lawrence River

Cranberry Lake

ADIRONDACK

Watertown

Stillwater Reservoir

Raquette Lake

NEW

YORK

MOUNTAINS

Lake George

Oswego

Oneida Lake

Rome

Great Sacandaga Reservoir

Mohawk River

Syracuse

Utica

Amsterdam

Schenectady

Troy

Auburn

BASEBALL HALL OF FAME

Albany ★

Cayuga Lake

Cooperstown

Seneca Lake

Ithaca

APPALACHIAN MOUNTAINS

CATSKILL

Elmira

Binghamton

MOUNTAINS

Woodstock

Hudson River

HOME OF FRANKLIN D. ROOSEVELT

Kingston

Delaware River

Hyde Park

Poughkeepsie

Newburgh

U.S. MILITARY ACADEMY

West Point

NEW JERSEY

White Plains

Long Island Sound

Montauk

Long Island

Yonkers

Mt. Vernon

SAGAMORE HILL (home of "Teddy" Roosevelt)

Southampton

New York City

UNITED NATIONS

Massapequa

Staten Island

ATLANTIC OCEAN

VERMONT

CONNECTICUT

▲ Historical Sites and Points of Interest

New York State farmers grow many varieties of apples. The apples are sold throughout the United States.

worth of trinkets. The Dutch built a village, New Amsterdam, on the southern tip of the island. More Dutch villages grew up in northern Manhattan, on Long Island, and up the Hudson. (*See* **New York City**.)

British colonists began settling in the Hudson Valley and on Long Island. French people from Canada settled in northern New York. In 1664, the British took New Amsterdam away from the Dutch and renamed it New York, in honor of the duke of York. For many years, the French and the Algonquian Indians fought against the British and the Iroquois. In 1763, the French were defeated and gave up their settlements.

During the American Revolution, many major battles were fought in New York. The British held New York City for most of the war, and encouraged the Iroquois Indians to attack upstate settlements. In 1779, soldiers defeated the Indians, opening up the western and northern areas for settlement.

The population of New York grew rapidly during the 1800s. In 1807, the first steamboat went up the Hudson from New York City to Albany. The Erie Canal was completed in 1825. It links Albany with Buffalo, on Lake Erie. People and goods could now travel across the state more easily and less expensively. (*See* **Erie Canal.**)

People New York has a mixture of people from all parts of the globe. Many have kept their own languages and customs.

Today, most New Yorkers live along the Hudson and Mohawk rivers and the Erie Canal. New York City is the largest city in the United States. Buffalo, Rochester, Yonkers, Syracuse, and Albany, are large cities, too.

New Yorkers of all backgrounds have helped George Washington's prediction come true. New York leads the nation, or comes close to leading it, in many fields. These include manufacturing, foreign trade, commerce, finance, publishing, theater, dance, and art. The chief industries are machinery, printing, clothing, and chemicals.

Agriculture is important to New York's economy. The state is famous for its apples, grapes, and cherries. A variety of other fruits and vegetables grow well, too. Dairy farming, winemaking, and raising beef cattle, hogs, and sheep are important.

Four presidents have come from New York—Martin Van Buren, Millard Fillmore, Theodore Roosevelt, and Franklin D. Roosevelt. (*See* **presidents of the United States.**)

New York City

New York is the largest city in the United States and one of the largest in the world. It is in the southeastern corner of New York State, where the Hudson River empties into the Atlantic Ocean.

Greater New York was created in 1898 when five boroughs—towns—joined together. The borough of Manhattan takes up Manhattan Island. People often refer to Manhattan alone as "New York." The Hudson River flows along the west side of Manhattan. The Harlem and East rivers are on the north and east sides.

The boroughs of Brooklyn and Queens lie across the East River from Manhattan, on Long Island. The Bronx, another borough, is on the mainland, north of Manhattan and

The giant towers of the World Trade Center stand over New York City's Brooklyn Bridge at sunset (left). New Yorkers enjoy a spring afternoon in Central Park (right).

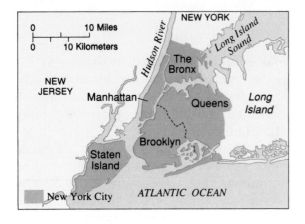

Queens. The fifth borough, Staten Island, is in New York Bay.

This great *metropolis*—large, important city—grew from a tiny Dutch village, New Amsterdam, on the southern tip of Manhattan Island. Settlers began to arrive around 1624. In 1626, the Dutch bought the island from the Canarsie Indians for trinkets worth about $24.

England gained control of New Amsterdam in 1664 and renamed it to honor the duke of York. Between 1785 and 1790, it served as the capital of the United States. It was the state capital until 1797.

The city expanded rapidly in the 1800s. The opening of the Erie Canal in 1825 helped bring people and trade to the city. Goods were shipped up the Hudson River and through the canal. New York's excellent harbor also helped the city grow.

Beginning in the 1800s, great numbers of Europeans moved to the United States. Many of them landed first in New York City. If they arrived after 1886, they passed the Statue of Liberty as they entered New York Bay. Immigrants who came after 1892 passed through the immigration receiving center on Ellis Island. (*See* **Statue of Liberty.**)

Many of the immigrants stayed in or near New York City. They have been joined by people from around the world. Throughout the five boroughs, there are neighborhoods where people from various countries have kept their own languages, customs, and foods.

Parts of New York City are very crowded, and many people who work in the city have moved to nearby cities and towns. Today, the New York metropolitan area—the city itself plus the communities that have grown up around it—is huge. It even includes some portions of Connecticut and New Jersey. Almost 18 million people live in or around New York City. That is more people than in all of the continent of Australia!

There are many ways of getting into and around New York City. You can reach almost any part of the city by subway, bus, or taxi. Underground walkways connect some of the larger office buildings. Highways, railroads, bridges, and tunnels link the boroughs and nearby cities. There are also ferries, airports, heliports, and a tramway!

The "Big Apple," as New York City is nicknamed, has an energy that few other cities can equal. John F. Kennedy International Airport is one of the busiest in the world. More ships come into New York's harbor than into any other port in the world. The city is a leading manufacturing center. Its chief industries are clothing, and printing and publishing. The nation's major television and radio networks have their headquarters there. The Wall Street district—at the southern tip of Manhattan—is the financial capital of the world. The United Nations has its headquarters in Manhattan.

New York is a great cultural and educational center, too. It is the art, music, and drama capital of the United States. Its museums, art galleries, libraries, zoos, and botanical gardens are world famous.

In New York City, you can see stately old buildings from colonial times and dramatic new ones by the world's best architects. You can look out over the whole metropolitan area from the top of the World Trade Center (110 stories tall) or from the Empire State Building (102 stories tall). You can see the newest plays and shows on Broadway. You can join the crowds that hurry along the narrow streets of the financial district. Or you can sit quietly and people-watch in one of the city's many parks. You can even ride a horse-drawn carriage through Manhattan's 840-acre (336-hectare) Central Park.

New Zealand

Capital: Wellington
Area: 103,736 square miles (268,676 square kilometers)
Population (1985): about 3,271,000
Official language: English

New Zealand is an island nation in the southwestern Pacific Ocean. A land of mountains, glaciers, waterfalls, and beaches, it is one of the most beautiful and peaceful nations in the world. Its nearest large neighbor, Australia, is more than 1,000 miles (1,609 kilometers) to the west.

New Zealand is made up of two large islands about 16 miles (22 kilometers) apart, and a handful of smaller islands in the South Pacific. The two main islands—the North Island and the South Island—stretch north and south for more than 1,000 miles (1,609 kilometers).

Most New Zealanders live on the North Island. The two largest cities—Auckland and Wellington, the capital—are there. Part of North Island was formed by volcanoes and still has some active volcanoes and geysers. The South Island has New Zealand's highest mountains and richest farmland.

Much of New Zealand is hilly, and is best suited for grazing animals. There are nearly

This hill outside Auckland is the cone of an extinct volcano.

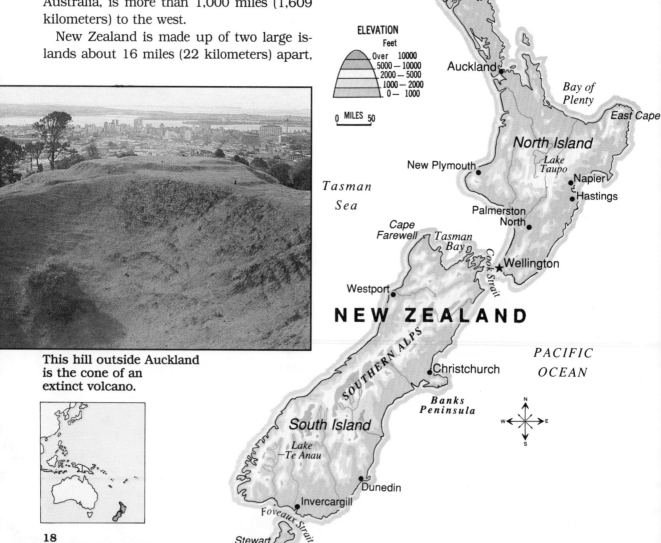

70 million sheep in New Zealand—more than 20 sheep per person! Dairy farming is important, too. New Zealand sells lamb, wool, cheese, and butter to other countries.

New Zealand is about the size of Colorado, with slightly more people. It is a prosperous nation with few very poor or very rich people. The government provides its citizens with many benefits, including one of the best public health programs in the world.

The first people to arrive in New Zealand were Maoris (MOW-reez). They came by canoe from other Pacific islands about 600 years ago. In the 1600s, Dutch explorers discovered the islands and named the place New Zealand, after a province in Holland. They left when the Maoris threatened them, and no other Europeans settled in New Zealand until the late 1700s.

The British built the first settlements in New Zealand and made it a British colony. New Zealand became independent of Britain, but it still belongs to the British Commonwealth. New Zealanders speak English and follow many British customs. They also enjoy British sports, such as cricket and rugby.

Niagara Falls

Every year, millions of tourists come to see Niagara Falls, one of the great natural wonders of the world. The falls are on the Niagara River, which flows north from Lake Erie to Lake Ontario. The river separates New York state from the province of Ontario.

Goat Island divides Niagara Falls into two waterfalls. Horseshoe Falls, on the Canadian side, drops 176 feet (54 meters) and is 2,215 feet (675 meters) wide. American Falls, on the United States' side, drops 184 feet (56 meters) and is 1,050 feet (320 meters) wide. Behind American Falls is a large cave called the Cave of the Winds.

Some of the water of the Niagara River never reaches the falls. It is channeled off to power hydroelectric plants. In the daytime during the tourist season, at least 100,000 cubic feet (2,830 cubic meters) per second

Visitors, protected by raincoats from the spray, stand near the foot of Niagara.

crashes down over the falls—most of it over Horseshoe Falls. The rest is used by hydroelectric power plants on the river.

Niagara Falls is slowly moving upstream toward Lake Erie. The force of the water is wearing away the ledge of Horseshoe Falls at about 3 inches (8 centimeters) a year. The ledge of American Falls is wearing away at about 1 inch (2.5 centimeters) a year.

Nicaragua, *see* Central America

nickel

The element nickel is a whitish metal. It is used most often in *alloys*—blends of metals. A U.S. five-cent coin is called a "nickel" even though it is three-fourths copper and one-fourth nickel. (*See* **alloy.**)

Nickel does not tarnish or corrode easily. It can be hammered into a thin sheet or stretched into a long, thin wire. It is magnetic, and can be polished to a shine. Nickel melts at 1,452° C (2,646° F).

Half of the nickel mined each year is blended with iron to make steel. The nickel makes the steel easy to shape. It makes the steel strong and resistant to rust. The nickel alloy is used to make chemical tanks and machine parts. (*See* **steel.**)

Turbine blades in jet engines are made from a nickel-chromium-iron alloy. The nickel helps the alloy resist high temperatures. Nickel alloys are also used in permanent magnets (nickel-cobalt-iron), and for some batteries (nickel-cadmium).

Canada holds about three-fourths of the world's supply of nickel. The Soviet Union, New Caledonia, Australia, and Cuba also have large deposits of nickel.

Niger, *see* Africa

Nigeria

Capital: Lagos
Area: 356,667 square miles (923,768 square kilometers)
Population (1985): about 102,783,000
Official language: English

Nigeria is a nation in western Africa. It has about as much land as the states of Texas and Oklahoma put together, but it has nearly five times as many people. With more than 100 million people, it has the largest population of any nation in Africa.

Land Nigeria is near the equator. Most of the country is warm year-round. The grasslands in the north are good for grazing animals. In the south, especially near the sea, rains are heavy. In some places, there are dense rain forests.

Nigeria's most important river is the Niger, which runs south through the eastern regions. It forms a huge, fan-shaped delta of soil where it flows into the Atlantic Ocean. (*See* **delta.**)

Most of Nigeria's land is fertile and can produce enough food for its growing population. Nigerians mine tin and other metals to sell to other countries. Petroleum is Nigeria's most important product. It was discovered in the 1960s in the Niger delta. Since then, Nigeria has become a major oil-producing country. Money from oil has made many changes in the country.

People Almost all Nigerians are black Africans. Most speak English, the nation's official language, but there are many differences among the people.

For hundreds of years, many different groups or tribes lived in the region that is

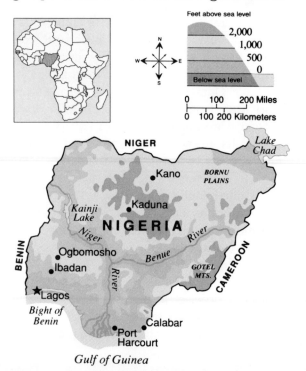

now Nigeria. These groups still speak their own languages. They do not trust people from other groups. The three largest groups are the Hausa, the Yoruba, and the Ibo. The Hausa live mainly in the north. The Yoruba live in the southwest, near the sea. The Ibo live in the east.

About half the people of Nigeria are Muslims—followers of Islam. About one-third are Christians. Many Nigerians mix ideas from Islam or Christianity with their traditional beliefs.

About three-quarters of all Nigerians live in small villages. Most live in homes made of grass, mud, or wood, with roofs of metal or straw. They have no running water or electricity. Both men and women wear loose robes made of light fabric. This clothing is comfortable to wear in the warm, humid climate. Most people living in the countryside work on farms.

People in the cities may live in modern apartment buildings. But many other people live in shacks around the edges of the cities. City people wear clothing much like that worn in Europe and the United States.

Lagos is Nigeria's capital and largest city. It is the main center of Nigerian business and industry. Money from the sale of oil has

These Muslims are going to pray in a mosque in the northern city of Kano.

helped Lagos grow into a busy, modern city. It is now one of the five largest cities in Africa.

History Little is known about the ancient history of Nigeria, because there are few written records. However, tools, human skeletons, clay sculpture, and rock paintings found in the region date back thousands of years.

Between the years 1000 and 1400, the Hausa began small kingdoms in the north of the region. In the south, the Yoruba tribe was most powerful. Many people became Muslims when missionaries brought Islam from North Africa.

In the late 1400s, the Portuguese began exploring Africa's western coast. They set up a trading center along the coast of Nigeria. Soon, other European traders arrived. Their main business was to buy slaves and carry them off to the Americas and other parts of the world.

The British became the leading slave traders. After Britain ended its slave trade in 1807, British traders remained in West Africa. In 1861, they made Lagos a British colony, and added other parts of Nigeria to their possessions. By the early 1900s, Britain claimed all of Nigeria.

Nigerians began demanding independence in the 1920s. Finally, in 1960, Nigeria became a country. Within a few years, different groups began to fight for control of the government. In the 1960s, Nigerians fought a bitter civil war. The eastern region wanted to become a separate nation. Thousands died in battle or from starvation. In the end, the Nigerian government won the war and kept the nation together.

Nigeria is one of the most prosperous countries in Africa. But compared to countries in North America and Europe, it is still very poor. Only about a fourth of the adults can read or write. Many farmers have only a few acres of land and find it hard to raise enough food for their families. But the government is working to bring Nigerians a better standard of living.

Florence Nightingale (above right) led a group of nurses who cared for injured soldiers. Her work improved the care that people received in hospitals.

Nightingale, Florence

Florence Nightingale was an English nurse. She dedicated herself to improving the care of sick and injured people. She is known as the founder of modern nursing.

Florence Nightingale was born in 1820 to a wealthy English family. She was named for the city of Florence, Italy, where her parents were living when she was born. As a young girl, she enjoyed caring for hurt animals and looking after children. When she was older, she decided to become a nurse. At this time, only a few women worked outside of the home. Hospitals were often dirty places, and many nurses worked while they were drunk. Nightingale's parents would not allow her to work in a hospital, but she was determined. She went to France and studied in a hospital there.

When Nightingale returned to England, she began working at a women's hospital in London. In 1854, Britain went to war against Russia. Most of the fighting took place in the Crimea, an area of southern Russia that juts out into the Black Sea. Sick and wounded British soldiers were sent to nearby Turkey. The British secretary of war asked Nightingale to lead a group of nurses there to help the injured soldiers.

The buildings used for the hospital were full of fleas and rats, and there were no beds. There was very little water. Nightingale quickly had the hospital cleaned and ordered supplies from England. She worked long hours during the day and walked the hospital's halls by night to look after the sick. Because of this, the soldiers called her the "lady with the lamp." While visiting soldiers on the battlefield, Nightingale caught a fever and almost died. Friends urged her to return to England, but she stayed until the end of the war.

When Florence Nightingale returned to England, she was a national heroine. People gave money to a fund in her honor. She used this money to start the Nightingale School for Nurses—the first school of its kind in the world.

For the rest of her life, Nightingale hardly ever left her home. Her health had been damaged by the fever and hard work. Even at home, Nightingale kept busy. She wrote letters and met with people from many countries, including the United States. Her efforts led to improved medical care, decent living quarters, and better food for British soldiers.

Nightingale was the first woman to be awarded the British Order of Merit. She died in 1910.

Nile River

The Nile is the world's longest river. It flows north through northeastern Africa to the Mediterranean Sea. At Cairo, Egypt, where it empties into the Mediterranean, the Nile forms a broad *delta*—deposits of fertile soil left behind by the river. From its beginning to its broad delta, the river is more than 4,100 miles (6,600 kilometers) long.

The longest portion of the Nile runs through the Sudan and Egypt. Most of the people of these countries live within a few miles of the river. It is their main source of water for farming. It is also a major highway, carrying thousands of small boats and large ships. Today, dams along the Nile also produce electricity.

The Nile's most distant source is in the country of Burundi. As it flows north, the small stream swells with water from Tanzania, Rwanda, Kenya, Uganda, and Zaire. In the southern Sudan, it winds through a giant swamp called the Sudd. When it comes out of the Sudd, it is called the White Nile.

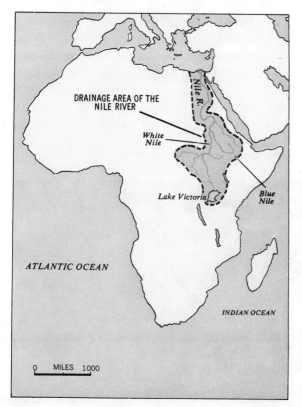

DRAINAGE AREA OF THE NILE RIVER

Nile R.

White Nile

Lake Victoria

Blue Nile

ATLANTIC OCEAN

INDIAN OCEAN

0   MILES   1000

At Khartoum, capital of the Sudan, the White Nile is met by a major *tributary*—a river that flows into it. This tributary is the Blue Nile. It begins in Ethiopia. North of Khartoum, the White Nile and the Blue Nile join to become the Nile. The giant river makes a huge S-shaped turn before it reaches Egypt. There are also several *cataracts*—large rapids—on the Nile.

The plains along the banks of the Nile are among the world's most productive farming regions. The river's waters are used to irrigate more than 10 million acres of farmland in Egypt and the Sudan. Farmers grow crops in rich soil left by the river's floods. These floods come each year in early summer, when the river waters are high from rains and melting snows. The area where rich soil deposits are left is called the *floodplain*. Beyond the floodplain, most of the land is very dry.

The rich soil is the main reason that ancient Egyptians settled along the Nile about 5,000 years ago. They called the land Kemet—"Black Land"—and built a great irrigation system to water their crops. Canals from the river brought water to inland fields.

In 1968, Egypt finished building the great Aswan High Dam. The dam makes it possible for farmers downstream to grow crops year-round. But the dam also keeps the rich soil from traveling down the river the way it used to. Farmers downstream must now use chemicals to enrich their soil.

nitrogen

The element nitrogen is a colorless, odorless, tasteless gas. It makes up four-fifths of the earth's atmosphere. All living things need nitrogen, but most of them cannot use nitrogen gas. They need *nitrogen compounds* —nitrogen that is chemically bonded with other elements. Humans and animals get nitrogen by eating other animals and plants. Plants get nitrogen from the soil.

One way nitrogen enters the soil is in rain and snow. Lightning makes the nitrogen

Bacteria in the bumps on these clover roots help put nitrogen into the soil.

and oxygen in the air combine. Rain and snow then bring these nitrogen compounds to the earth.

Nitrogen compounds are also made by plants. Plants in the legume family—clover, beans, and peas—have bumps called *nodules* on their roots. Nitrogen-fixing bacteria inside the nodules combine nitrogen gas with other elements to form nitrogen compounds. When the plants die, the nitrogen compounds are released into the soil. New plants use these nitrogen compounds to grow. This continuous circle—from atmosphere to rain to soil to plants to animals, and so on—is called the *nitrogen cycle.*

Since plants need nitrogen, most plant fertilizers contain some form of nitrogen. Nitrogen compounds have other uses. Household ammonia, which is often used for cleaning, is a compound containing nitrogen. Some dentists use nitrous oxide—"laughing gas" —as an anesthetic.

Nixon, Richard M.

Richard Milhous Nixon was the 37th president of the United States. He served from 1969 to 1974, and was the only president to give up the office before his term was over. During Nixon's years as president, the United States ended its part in the Vietnam War and reopened contact with the People's Republic of China.

Nixon was born in 1913 in Yorba Linda, California. He attended Whittier College and earned a law degree from Duke University. Running as a Republican, Nixon won election to the U.S. House of Representatives in 1946. In 1950, he was elected to the U.S. Senate. He served as vice president under President Dwight D. Eisenhower from 1953 to 1961. Nixon ran for president in 1960 against John F. Kennedy. It was one of the closest presidential races in history. Nixon lost, but he ran again and won in 1968.

Nixon was easily reelected in 1972. During that presidential campaign, some of his supporters did illegal things. They broke into the headquarters of the Democratic party at the Watergate buildings in Washington, D.C. Nixon resigned and returned to

During his visit to China in 1972, President Richard Nixon (right) sits next to Chinese leader Zhou Enlai at a banquet in Shanghai.

private life before Congress could accuse him of knowing about these acts and trying to cover them up.

See also **Vietnam War** and **China**.

Nobel Prize

Nobel Prizes are awards given each year to men and women whose work has given something important to the world and its people. The prizes are awarded in six categories—peace, physics, chemistry, medicine, literature, and economics. Sometimes, the award is given for a specific achievement. For example, a Nobel Prize in medicine was given for the discovery of vitamin K. In the field of literature, the Nobel Prize is given for a lifetime of work. A prize may be awarded to one person or shared by several people. Prizes may be given to organizations, such as the Red Cross.

The idea for these prizes came from Alfred Nobel, a Swedish scientist and manufacturer. In 1867, he invented an explosive, which he called *dynamite.* The demand for dynamite was great, and Nobel set up many dynamite factories. Within a few years, he became very rich. Nobel had invented dynamite for peaceful uses, such as building roads. Instead, he saw dynamite used as a weapon in wartime. Nobel felt ashamed and guilty that his invention caused destruction.

Before he died, Nobel asked that his money be used to award prizes each year to people who helped humanity. He provided for awards in physics, chemistry, literature, medicine, and peace. The first awards were made in 1901. A sixth field, economics, was added later. The first Nobel Prize in economics was awarded in 1969.

Awarding the Prizes The Nobel Prize winners are chosen by four organizations. The Royal Academy of Science, in Stockholm, Sweden, awards the prizes in physics, chemistry, and economics. The Caroline Institute, also in Stockholm, awards the prize in medicine. The Swedish Academy of Literature, in Stockholm, awards the prize in

A Nobel Prize winner receives a certificate (above), a medal, and a large cash prize.

literature. A committee elected by the Norwegian parliament chooses the peace prize winner. Individuals write to the committees and suggest the names of people they think deserve prizes. The committee members spend months reviewing the names. They study each person's career and the contributions he or she has made to a particular field.

The committees make their decisions in the fall. The prizes are given in December. Winners of the peace prize receive their awards in Oslo, Norway. The other winners receive their prizes in Stockholm, Sweden.

Each winner is awarded a gold medal, a diploma, and money. In the late 1980s, the cash prize for each award was more than $200,000. This amount is shared if there are two or three winners in a field.

Some awards are not given every year. For example, no peace prize was given during most of World War II. Awards are sometimes refused by an individual or by a nation. The first person to turn down a Nobel Prize was Gerhard Domagk, a German scientist, in 1939. Domagk had discovered sulfa drugs. Adolf Hitler, Germany's ruler, forbade Domagk to accept his Nobel Prize. In such a case, the person is still considered the winner, but receives no money.

Sometimes, winners are forbidden to collect their awards. Andrei Sakharov was the first person from the Soviet Union to win the peace prize. He won the award in 1975 for his work for human rights. The government of the Soviet Union did not allow him to go to Oslo, so his wife, Elena Bonner, accepted the award for him.

Some Winners and Their Prizes Marie Curie, a Polish-born French scientist, was the first woman to receive a Nobel Prize. She shared the physics award in 1903 with her husband, Pierre, and Antoine Henri Becquerel. Curie also became the first person to win a second Nobel prize—in chemistry, in 1911. The Curies' daughter, Irène Joliot-Curie, won the chemistry prize in 1935, along with her husband, Frédéric.

The first father-and-son winners came from Denmark. Niels Bohr won the physics prize in 1922. His son Aage—along with two other scientists—received the physics award in 1975.

President Theodore Roosevelt was the first American to win a Nobel Prize. He was given the peace award in 1906 for helping to arrange a peace treaty between Russia and Japan. Woodrow Wilson was another U.S. president to win a Nobel Prize. Wilson won the peace award in 1919 for his work on the treaty that ended World War I, and for his idea of a League of Nations.

Ralph Bunche, also an American, was the first black to win a peace prize. He received the award in 1950 after working out a peace agreement between Israel and its Arab neighbors.

In 1964, Martin Luther King, Jr., became the youngest person to win a Nobel Prize. King, a leader of the black civil rights movement in the United States, won the Nobel Prize for peace at age 35.

Many Nobel winners use their prize money to continue their work. Some winners have given their money away. King gave his cash award to the civil rights movement. Mother Teresa of Calcutta, who won the peace prize in 1979, has used her award to extend her work with poor people all over the world. A Canadian doctor, Sir Frederick Banting, was given the 1923 prize in medicine for the discovery of *insulin,* a hormone used to treat diabetes. Banting believed that Charles Best, a doctor who worked with him, also deserved an award. So Banting gave Best half the prize money.

See also **Addams, Jane; Churchill, Sir Winston; Curie, Marie and Pierre; Einstein, Albert; King, Martin Luther, Jr.; Roosevelt, Theodore;** and **United Nations.**

Yuan T. Lee (left), won a Nobel Prize in chemistry for scientific research.
Mother Teresa (right), a nun who helped the poor of the world, won a peace prize.

Nomads in a dry region of Africa tend their animals at a water hole. Humans and animals move from place to place to find food and water.

nomad

A nomad is a person who keeps moving from place to place. People with a nomadic way of life have no permanent home, but they do stay within a certain large area.

Some nomads move every few days or weeks. Others move once or twice a year. Among some peoples, only the younger men live as nomads, while the women, children, and old people remain in one place. Most nomads live and travel in small groups—perhaps two or three families together. They do not have many belongings. If they did, moving would be too difficult.

Ancient Nomads People have lived as nomads much longer than they have lived a settled life. Early people depended on wild animals and plants for their basic needs. They hunted animals for meat, furs, and skins. They gathered fruit, leaves, roots, and seeds for food. They made simple shelters from leaves and branches. When the resources in one area were used up, people moved to a new area to find fresh supplies. Sometimes they followed migrating animals.

Nomads like these are called *hunter-gatherers.*

When early people learned to grow crops, many became farmers and settled near their fields. Living in one place was easier than living as a nomad. But not everyone became a farmer. Many people continued to live as nomads. Nomads still live in many areas of the world.

Nomads Who Hunt and Gather Some American Indian tribes once lived as nomads. The Sioux and the Cheyenne hunted the buffalo, following the large herds that used to live on the Great Plains of Canada and the United States. The aborigines of Australia hunted kangaroos and smaller creatures. The Eskimo of the Far North hunted whales, seals, caribou, and fish. The nomadic way of life has almost ended for descendants of these peoples today. (*See* **aborigines; Eskimo;** and **Indians, American.**)

About 50,000 Bushmen live today in the Kalahari Desert of southwestern Africa. They wander over the hot, dry land searching for food. The men use bows and arrows to kill animals ranging in size from tortoises to antelopes. The women find plants, especially melons, roots, and nuts. They use the shells of ostrich eggs for storing and carrying water. Whoever finds food shares it with the rest of the group. The Bushmen share most of their possessions—bows and arrows, knives, cooking pots, and jewelry.

When the Bushmen stop at a campsite, the women build small huts of branches and leaves. This takes them about two hours. When the band moves on after a few days or weeks, they leave the huts behind.

Nomads Who Herd Animals People became nomadic herders when they learned to *domesticate*—tame—animals. They led their herds of cattle, sheep, goats, or camels to water and grasslands. After the animals had drunk their fill or eaten most of the grass, the nomads would take them to a new area.

Today, several groups of nomads herd animals. They get meat, milk, hides, and wool from their animals. Many nomadic herders also use their animals for trade. For example, a sheepherder might trade mutton and wool in exchange for flour, sugar, tea, vegetables, or metal tools.

The Masai are a group of herders who live in Kenya and Tanzania, in Africa. Each family has its own herd of cattle. The Masai get milk from their cattle and consider them special creatures. They name their cattle, decorate them, and write songs and poems about them. Important occasions—such as birth, marriage, and death—are marked by giving cattle.

The bedouin are nomadic Arabs of North Africa and the Middle East. They herd camels and sheep across the deserts in search of *oases*. An oasis has a spring or water well and usually some trees. Bedouin families live in big woolen tents. They roll up their tents and load them onto camels when they move.

In parts of Mongolia in eastern Asia, nomadic herders still follow the ways of their ancestors. They live in small felt tents called *yurts* and use sturdy ponies to move their animals from place to place.

See also **Gypsies.**

Normandy

Normandy is the part of northwestern France that faces the English Channel. It has played an important part in European history for hundreds of years.

During the 800s, Normandy was invaded by warriors from northern Europe. These were the Vikings, or *Norsemen.* The Norsemen built settlements and ruled the area. Normandy was named for the Norsemen's descendants, the Normans. (*See* **Vikings.**)

In 1066, the Norman leader William the Conqueror led a group of soldiers across the English Channel. William defeated the English army at the Battle of Hastings. He was crowned king of England in 1066. (*See* **William the Conqueror.**)

William's son, Henry I, ruled over a united kingdom of England and Normandy. France fought England for control of Normandy during the Hundred Years' War. In 1449, the French won, and the region became part of France.

One of the most important battles of World War II took place in Normandy. On June 6, 1944—later known as D day—American general Dwight D. Eisenhower led English and United States forces across the English Channel to Normandy. From there, they were later able to force the German army out of France. (*See* **World War II.**)

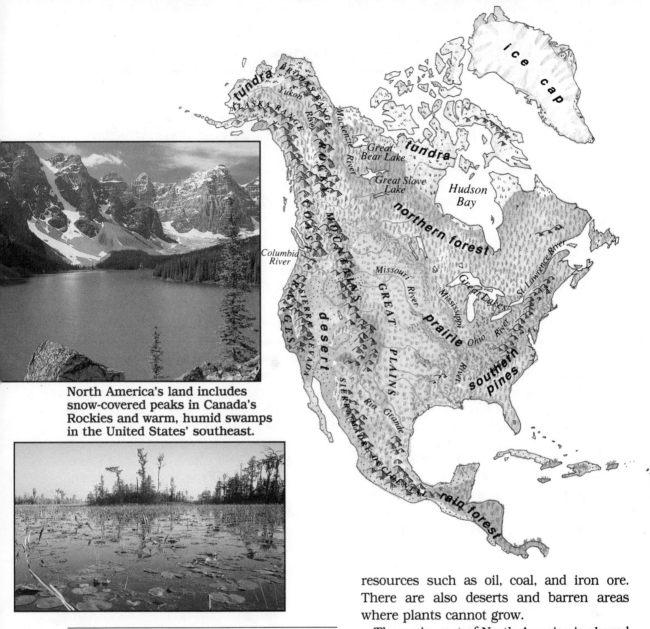

North America's land includes snow-covered peaks in Canada's Rockies and warm, humid swamps in the United States' southeast.

North America

North America is one of the earth's seven continents—major bodies of land. It covers more than 9 million square miles (23.3 million square kilometers). North America is the third-largest continent. Asia and Africa are larger.

North America is a land of tremendous variety. In the Far North, toward the North Pole, temperatures are below freezing for most of the year. In the South, toward the equator, the weather is hot year-round.

North America has high mountains and vast open plains. Much of the land is rich, producing food crops, timber, and mineral resources such as oil, coal, and iron ore. There are also deserts and barren areas where plants cannot grow.

The main part of North America is shared by only three countries—Canada, the United States, and Mexico. The continents of South America, Asia, Europe, and Africa each have many countries.

Three other regions are sometimes included as part of North America. One of these is Central America, the thin stretch of land that connects North America and South America. A second is made up of the island countries of the West Indies in the Caribbean Sea. A third area sometimes included in North America is Greenland, a large island off the northeast coast of Canada. For more information on these regions, *see* **Central America; West Indies;** and **Greenland.**

NORTH AMERICAN COUNTRIES

Country	Capital	Square Miles	Square Kilometers	Population
Canada	Ottawa	3,851,790	9,976,136	25,399,000
Mexico	Mexico City	761,601	1,972,547	79,662,000
United States	Washington, D.C.	3,615,105	9,363,122	238,631,000
TOTAL		8,228,496	21,311,805	343,692,000

Land North America is surrounded by three oceans. To the east is the Atlantic Ocean. To the west is the Pacific Ocean. To the north is the Arctic Ocean, most of which is frozen all year. The Gulf of Mexico and the Caribbean Sea—arms of the Atlantic Ocean—separate North and South America.

The "spine" of North America is made of vast mountain systems. They run from Alaska in the North through western Canada, the United States, and Mexico, and then into Central America.

Canada and the United States stretch thousands of miles across, between the Pacific and Atlantic oceans. Together, these two countries take up more than nine-tenths of the mainland of North America.

To see the great variety of the land, imagine you are in a spacecraft traveling slowly from West to East across the continent. You begin your journey over a narrow strip of land between the Pacific Ocean and the coastal mountain ranges. Millions of people live in this narrow strip. In the United States, California is the state with the most people in this region.

Then you are over mountains. The peaks of the Pacific Coast System run north and south. These mountain ranges include the Sierra Madre Occidental in Mexico, the Sierra Nevada in California, the Cascade Mountains in Washington, Canada's Coast Mountains, and the Alaska Range in Alaska. Mount McKinley, in the Alaska Range, is the highest point in North America.

Continuing east past the mountains, you come to a rugged section of *plateaus*—high, flat land—smaller mountains, and flat basins. This region includes the Yukon River Basin in Alaska and Canada, the Great Basin in the western United States, the Colorado Plateau, and the Mexican Plateau. The continent's lowest point is in Death Valley, in the Great Basin.

Still traveling east, you find yourself over a wide system of mountains that runs north and south from the Arctic Ocean to Mexico. In Canada and the United States, this system forms the Rocky Mountains. The part of this mountain system that is in Mexico is called the Sierra Madre Oriental. Several Rocky Mountain peaks are more than 14,000 feet (4,270 meters) above sea level.

As you pass over the Rockies and continue east, you see the land leveling off. You are approaching the central region of North America—the Great Plains. The Great Plains stretch from central Canada to the state of Texas. The land nearest the Rockies may look rather brown and dry. As you travel east, the land becomes greener, because it gets more rain.

Now you are over gently rolling hills. This rolling country with rich, black soil is the prairie. Most of North America's food is grown in these plains and prairie regions.

In the middle of the prairies, you may see broad, deep rivers. Nearly all these rivers eventually flow into the Mississippi River. The broad, deep Mississippi flows south into the Gulf of Mexico.

Just east and north of the Mississippi are the Great Lakes—five large freshwater lakes. All but Lake Michigan are shared by the United States and Canada. Lake Superior is the largest freshwater lake in the world.

Still farther north, there is an even larger body of water. This is Hudson Bay, an arm of the Atlantic Ocean that reaches down into central Canada. Surrounding Hudson Bay are ancient rock formations that are among the oldest ever discovered.

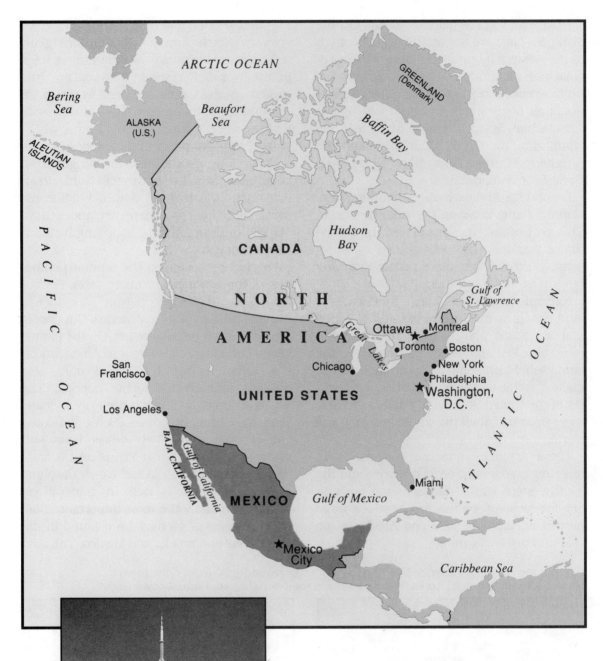

The CN Tower in Toronto is the highest
free-standing structure in the world.
It stands 1,815 feet (544 meters) high.
There is a restaurant near the top.

Up ahead, you see more mountains in the distance. They are not as rugged or as high as the western mountains. These are the Appalachian Mountains. They stretch from the St. Lawrence River in Canada to the state of Alabama. Many smaller ranges make up the Appalachian System. They include the White Mountains, the Green Mountains, and the Allegheny, Cumberland, Blue Ridge, and Great Smoky mountains.

Beyond the Appalachians is another plain, sloping gently down to the Atlantic Ocean. This part of eastern Canada and the United States was the first to be settled by Europeans. Today, it has more people than any other part of the continent.

Natural Resources North America is a land rich in natural resources. It has varied and abundant plant life, animal life, and minerals. Perhaps most important is the land itself. Much of it receives enough rain to make it fertile farmland. Together, the farmers of the United States and Canada produce more than half of all the wheat grown in the world.

There are also immense wastelands. A huge region covering central Mexico and the southwestern United States is too hot and dry for farming. In the Far North, a large part of northern Canada and Alaska is too cold and dry for farming.

Thousands of different plants and trees grow in North America. California's giant redwoods and sequoias are the largest trees in the world. Forests in Canada and the United States provide the world with one-quarter of its lumber. They also provide half the world's supply of wood pulp, which is used to make paper and cardboard.

North America's animal life ranges from polar bears, who live in the cold North, to alligators in the tropical South. Wildlife experts estimate that there are more than 10,000 kinds of animals, including birds, in North America.

People have changed the animal population of the continent in many ways. For example, the passenger pigeon was once a common bird in eastern America. But people hunted it until none were left. On the plains, people killed large numbers of American bison (often called buffalo). People also brought animals to North America. The Spanish brought tame sheep and goats. They also brought horses. Some got loose and became wild. Their descendants still roam parts of the Great Plains and islands off the shore of Virginia and North Carolina.

North America is rich in mineral resources. Probably the most important is oil. Huge reserves of oil have been found in the United States, Canada, and Mexico. The land

The people of North America live in a variety of surroundings, from downtown Mexico City (below left), to California suburbs (below right), to a small town (right).

beneath the Appalachian Mountains holds perhaps the world's largest deposits of coal. Canada and the United States together mine about one-sixth of the world's iron ore, which is used in making steel. Mexico is the world's leading producer of silver. Other useful minerals found in North America include copper, uranium, zinc, and gold. Spanish explorers and the early settlers of California, northwestern Canada, and Alaska all came looking for gold.

People The earliest people in North America came from Asia at least 20,000 years ago. They came across land that used to connect Siberia and Alaska. Some of these peoples traveled south into North America and spread across the continent. Over many years, they moved into Central and South America. They are the ancestors of all American Indian tribes. (*See* **Indians, American; Aztec; Maya;** and **Inca.**)

The ancestors of the Eskimo sailed from Asia to North America about 6,000 years ago. They settled in Alaska, Canada, and Greenland. (*See* **Eskimo.**)

Probably the first European to arrive in North America was Leif Ericson. This Viking explorer landed on the shore of eastern Canada around the year 1000. But he did not stay, and most Europeans never learned about his discoveries.

North America was discovered again by Christopher Columbus in the 1490s, when he was exploring for Spain. Soon, other explorers and settlers were arriving on the continent. The Spanish set up colonies in the West Indies, South America, Central America, and parts of North America—Mexico, and what is now Florida and the U.S. West and Southwest. Today, many of these regions are made up of independent countries, but Spanish is often still the main language. (*See* **explorers.**)

In the late 1500s, the French and English began exploring the eastern shore of the continent. By the early 1600s, they were sending people to settle there. Both countries made colonies of the regions they settled. French is still the main language in eastern Canada, and English is the main language in the rest of Canada and the United States.

About one person in ten in North America is black. Nearly all black people are descendants of Africans who were brought to the continent as slaves. In recent years, many people from Asia have also settled in North America. These include people of Chinese, Korean, Japanese, and Vietnamese heritage. In the United States and Canada, about one person out of every 100 is an American Indian. But in Mexico, about 30 people out of every 100 are Indians, and most of the rest are *mestizos*—people of mixed Indian and Spanish heritage.

North America is sometimes called a "melting pot" of people from different cultures. Citizens of Canada, the United States, and Mexico think of themselves as Canadians, Americans, or Mexicans, but many maintain their own ethnic customs, too.

See also **Canada; United States;** and **Mexico.**

North Carolina

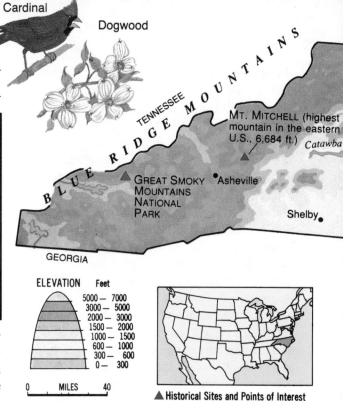

Cardinal

Dogwood

Capital: Raleigh
Area: 52,669 square miles (136,413 square kilometers) (28th-largest state)
Population (1980): 5,890,415 (1985): about 6,255,000 (10th-largest state)
Became a state: November 21, 1789 (12th state)

ELEVATION Feet

5000 —	7000
3000 —	5000
2000 —	3000
1500 —	2000
1000 —	1500
600 —	1000
300 —	600
0 —	300

0   MILES   40

▲ Historical Sites and Points of Interest

North Carolina is a southern state on the Atlantic coast of the United States. It is bordered on the north by Virginia, on the south by South Carolina and Georgia, and on the west by Tennessee.

North Carolina has beautiful beaches, fine farmland, and rugged mountains. Yet this state is as well known for its thriving manufacturing businesses as for its beauty and natural resources.

Land North Carolina's narrow western end is high in the Appalachian Mountains. Its eastern end opens out onto coastal lowlands. The lowlands take up almost half of the state. Just beyond the shore lie the *outer banks*—long, narrow islands that protect the mainland from the Atlantic's storms.

The storms and rapidly changing shorelines have caused about 700 shipwrecks in the area. One stretch of the outer banks, Cape Hatteras, is so dangerous that it is called the "Graveyard of the Atlantic." The pirate Edward Teach, known as "Blackbeard," used the outer banks as a hideout. He was finally caught, but no one ever found his treasure.

The western half of the coastal lowland has the state's best farmland. Farming is also excellent in the Piedmont—the rolling hills that lie between the lowlands and the Appalachian Mountains. The Piedmont's swift-flowing rivers have long provided power for mills and factories.

The Blue Ridge Mountains and the Great Smoky Mountains are Appalachian ranges that cross North Carolina. Mount Mitchell, the tallest peak in the eastern United States, is in the Great Smokies. It is 6,643 feet (1,993 meters) high.

History When Europeans arrived in the area in the 1500s, they found Indians from 30 different tribes living there.

In 1585, Sir Walter Raleigh started the first English colony in the New World on Roanoke Island, now part of North Carolina. The colony failed. Another one was started there in 1587. One year later, the entire colony vanished. One of the people who belonged to this "Lost Colony" was a baby girl named Virginia Dare—the first child of English parents to be born in America.

The first successful Carolina settlement was started in the 1650s by English people who came from Virginia. They were soon joined by families from other colonies. This pattern of settlement was different from that in the other, older colonies, where settlers came directly from Europe. So many settlers came to Carolina that the southern part of the area was made into a separate colony, South Carolina, in 1712.

Map labels:
Yadkin River · Reidsville · John H. Kerr Reservoir · SITE OF WRIGHT BROTHERS' FIRST SUCCESSFUL AIRPLANE FLIGHT, DECEMBER 17, 1903 · Elizabeth City · Kitty Hawk · Greensboro · Burlington · Chowan River · Roanoke River · Albemarle Sound · Nags Head · Winston-Salem · Chapel Hill · Durham · Rocky Mount · River · Statesville · High Point · UNIVERSITY OF NORTH CAROLINA · ★Raleigh · Wilson · FORT RALEIGH NATIONAL HISTORIC SITE · Roanoke Island · Salisbury · Lexington · High Rock Lake · Greenville · Lake Norman · N O R T H · Kannapolis · Badin Lake · Goldsboro · C A R O L I N A · Kinston · Pamlico Sound · Cape Hatteras · Gastonia · Concord · Neuse River · Charlotte · FORT BRAGG · Pee Dee River · New Bern · OUTER BANKS · Lake Wylie · Lake Wylie · Fayetteville · Raleigh Bay · Lumberton · Cape Fear River · CAMP LEJEUNE (Marine amphibious training base) · SOUTH CAROLINA · Onslow Bay · Wilmington · ATLANTIC OCEAN · Long Bay · Cape Fear

Wildflowers grow near Grandfather Mountain in western North Carolina.

North Carolina became a wealthy colony, and then a wealthy state. Tobacco was a leading crop, and a good deal of gold was mined. There were also cotton mills.

But the state suffered terribly during the Civil War, from 1861 to 1865. North Carolina joined the Confederate States of America. Tens of thousands of North Carolinians were killed. Farm fields became overgrown with weeds, and many buildings were destroyed or damaged.

People Today, North Carolina is a state of small towns and small farms. It is again a leader in several fields. It ranks number one among states in the production of tobacco, furniture, bricks, and textiles.

The chief crop is tobacco. Two-fifths of all the tobacco grown in the United States is grown in North Carolina. The value of the tobacco crop is greater than the value of all other North Carolina crops combined.

Cotton is the second-most important crop. Much of it is knitted or woven into textiles in North Carolina. The state is the home of the largest towel and denim mills in the world. Denim is the fabric from which jeans are made. If all of the denim produced every year in just one mill in Greensboro were unrolled, it would circle the world twice!

Some of the cotton is made into upholstery, the sturdy cloth that covers the furniture made in factories throughout the state.

Charlotte, North Carolina's largest city, is a manufacturing and trade center. Winston-Salem and Durham are tobacco and textile centers. Raleigh is the state capital.

In 1903, near a village called Kitty Hawk, Orville and Wilbur Wright made the world's first successful airplane flight. They chose the Kitty Hawk area on the outer banks because of its high sand dunes and sea breezes. Today, the Wright Brothers National Memorial and its museum attract visitors from all over the world.

Two United States presidents have come from North Carolina—James K. Polk (11th president) and Andrew Johnson (17th president). (*See* **presidents of the United States.**)

North Dakota

Capital: Bismarck
Area: 70,702 square miles (183,118 square kilometers) (17th-largest state)
Population (1980): 652,717 (1985): about 685,000 (46th-largest state)
Became a state: November 2, 1889 (39th state)

What is the tallest structure in the United States? It is not a skyscraper in Chicago or New York. It is a 2,063-foot (629-meter) television tower in the town of Blanchard, North Dakota!

North Dakota is a farm state in the north-central United States. It is bordered by Canada on the north, South Dakota on the south, Minnesota on the east, and Montana on the west. On a map, it looks like a rectangle at the very top of the nation.

Land The Red River flows north along the state's eastern border. The Red River Valley is a low, flat plain that rises gradually to hills and *buttes*—steep hills with flat tops. One of these, White Butte, is the highest spot in the state. It is 3,506 feet (1,069 meters) above sea level.

Summers are comfortably cool in North Dakota, but winters are bitterly cold, with freezing winds and plenty of snow. Fertile soil is North Dakota's major natural resource. Most of the state is covered with farms and ranches. The miles of grasslands are good for cattle to graze on.

North Dakota is a major wheat-producing state, second only to Kansas. Barley, oats, rye, and flax (used in making linen cloth and linseed oil) are also important crops. North Dakota uses more of its land for agriculture than does any other state.

There are few trees, except along riverbanks or where people have planted them as windbreaks beside fields and houses. Since there were no trees, early settlers built their houses and barns of *sod*—cubes of earth. Sod houses stayed warm in winter and cool in summer, but insects and leaks were sometimes problems.

The Missouri River flows southeastward through the west-central part of the state. Workers began building the Garrison Dam across the river in 1946. It began operating in 1956 but was not completed until 1960. This dam helps to control floods in the spring, when the snows melt. The dam has also created Lake Sakakawea, the second-largest artificial lake in the United States. The lake provides water for irrigating crops. It is a source of hydroelectric power, too. The northern end of the nation's largest artificial lake, Oahe, is also in North Dakota. (*See* **Missouri River.**)

North Dakota's land contains valuable resources. Farmers have long used windmills to bring water from large underground lakes to the surface. North Dakota also has the world's largest deposits of *lignite*—a kind of coal. Petroleum and natural gas were discovered in western North Dakota in 1951. Today, there are several oil refineries in the state.

History The area that is now North Dakota was inhabited by several tribes of Indians. In fact, the region is named for the Dakota Indians, who are also called Sioux.

In the 1700s, the Indians of western North Dakota trapped fur animals and sold the pelts to traders from French Canada. In 1803, the United States bought the area from France as part of the Louisiana Purchase. (*See* **Louisiana Purchase.**)

The British started to settle the Pembina Mountains region near the Red River Valley. In 1818, Great Britain agreed to give the United States what is now northeastern North Dakota and northwestern Minnesota. This included Pembina.

The fur trade remained important until about the middle of the 1800s. When Congress created the Dakota Territory, in 1861,

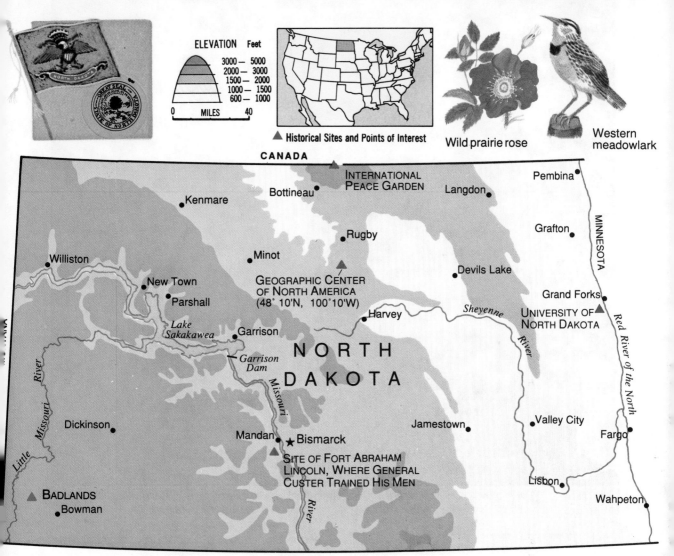

ELEVATION Feet

3000 —	5000
2000 —	3000
1500 —	2000
1000 —	1500
600 —	1000

0 — MILES — 40

▲ Historical Sites and Points of Interest

Wild prairie rose

Western meadowlark

CANADA

Kenmare

Bottineau

INTERNATIONAL PEACE GARDEN

Langdon

Pembina

Rugby

Grafton

Minot

Williston

GEOGRAPHIC CENTER OF NORTH AMERICA (48° 10'N, 100° 10'W)

Devils Lake

MINNESOTA

New Town

Parshall

Harvey

Sheyenne

Grand Forks

UNIVERSITY OF NORTH DAKOTA

Red River of the North

Lake Sakakawea

Garrison

River

NORTH

Garrison Dam

DAKOTA

Missouri

Dickinson

Jamestown

Valley City

Fargo

Little Missouri River

Mandan

★ Bismarck

SITE OF FORT ABRAHAM LINCOLN, WHERE GENERAL CUSTER TRAINED HIS MEN

Lisbon

BADLANDS

Bowman

River

Wahpeton

SOUTH DAKOTA

settlers began arriving. The government promised free land to *homesteaders*—people who would live on the land and improve it. Railroads were built across the state, and new ways of milling wheat were developed. Because of this, the demand for North Dakota's wheat increased.

In spite of the promise of free land, North Dakota grew slowly, partly because of the

North Dakota's land slowly rises to mountains in the west.

warfare between settlers and Indians. Government treaties with the Indians were broken by the settlers, causing new battles. Peace finally came when Chief Sitting Bull surrendered in 1881. (*See* **Sitting Bull.**)

People Even today, not many people live in North Dakota, and there are no large cities. Fargo, the biggest city in the state, is a railroad and trading center. The state capital is Bismarck, a medium-size trading center. Grand Forks—home of the state-owned flour mill and the state university—is the third-largest city.

Many of the people who settled North Dakota came from the Scandinavian countries, especially Norway. The second-largest group came from Germany. The descendants of these European settlers make up most of the population today.

The strange glow of the *aurora borealis*—northern lights—appears in northern skies at night. These northern lights were photographed near Fairbanks, Alaska.

Northern Ireland, *see* United Kingdom

northern lights

Northern lights are glowing patches of light that appear in the night sky. They are produced in the upper atmosphere. Another name for the lights is *aurora borealis*, which means "northern dawn." To see them, you generally must be close to the North Pole—in Alaska, Canada, Sweden, Norway, or Siberia. Sometimes, when conditions are right, the lights show up over the northern United States.

Northern lights take different shapes. Most often, they look like big curtains or rays. The lights may be steady, or may come and go in the same spot. The color of the light varies from whitish green to dark red. If the lights occur low in the atmosphere, they may appear orange.

Scientists think that northern lights are caused by particles from the sun entering the earth's atmosphere. The sun gives off a steady stream of particles—called the *solar wind.* The solar wind travels at very high speeds. When the speeding particles crash into the particles in the earth's atmosphere, they make the night sky glow. The same process goes on in the daytime, but the glow is not bright enough to show up in sunlight.

The electrically charged particles in the solar wind are drawn to the North Pole by Earth's magnetism. Earth's magnetism also draws particles to the South Pole, causing the same kind of lights. These are called *southern lights,* or *aurora australis.*

North Korea, *see* Korea

North Pole

If a step in any direction would be a step to the south, where are you? This could only happen if you were standing at the North Pole, the northernmost place on Earth.

A line straight down through Earth from the North Pole would come out at the South Pole. Imagining this line through the earth helps us understand some things about Earth. We call our imaginary line the earth's *axis*. The earth turns on its axis.

The North Pole is easy to find on a globe. First, it is at the top. Second, it is one of two places where all the map's *longitude* lines—all its north-to-south lines—meet. The other place they meet is at the South Pole. (*See* latitude and longitude.)

The North Pole is actually in the middle of the huge Arctic Ocean. But the ocean is frozen most of the year, so explorers trying to reach the Pole traveled to it over ice, on dogsleds. The first person to arrive at the Pole was the American explorer Robert Peary, who reached it in 1909. Another way to reach the North Pole is underwater. In 1958,

the nuclear submarine *Nautilus* reached the North Pole *under* the ice.

See also **South Pole; Peary, Robert E.; Amundsen, Roald;** and **Arctic regions.**

North Sea

The North Sea is an arm of the Atlantic Ocean. It is surrounded by Britain to the west, Denmark and Norway to the east, and France, Belgium, the Netherlands, and West Germany to the south. The North Sea has an area of about 220,000 square miles (568,800 square kilometers).

The North Sea has long been known for its savage storms. It is not as deep as other seas, and storm winds churn up shallow waters more easily. North Sea winds have often been measured at over 100 miles (160 kilometers) an hour. Wave heights have been known to reach higher than 90 feet (150 kilometers)! Yet the North Sea is an important trade and transportation route.

For centuries, fishing was the most important industry in the North Sea. Then, in 1970, rich deposits of petroleum and natural

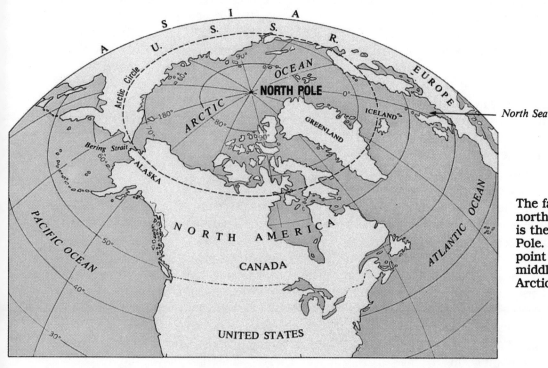

The farthest north you can go is the North Pole. It is a point in the middle of the Arctic Ocean.

gas were discovered beneath the seafloor. Companies from Norway and Great Britain built drilling platforms to pump out the oil. Today, oil and natural gas are the North Sea's most important products, and Norway and Great Britain have become important oil-producing nations.

North Star

The North Star appears almost directly above the earth's North Pole. As the earth rotates, all other heavenly bodies, including our sun and moon, move across the sky. When the seasons change and the earth tilts on its axis, their paths move north or south. But the North Star appears in the same place, night after night, season after season, year after year. The ancient Egyptians believed this unmoving star marked the way to a world of eternal life.

The North Star is also called Polaris. It can be seen on any clear night from any place north of the earth's equator. It is the last star on the Little Dipper's handle in the constellation Ursa Minor. It looks like a single bright star, but is really three stars close together. (*See* **constellation.**)

The North Star's steady position has been important for navigation. Sailors and explorers could tell the direction in which they were traveling by looking at the North Star. By knowing which way was north, they also knew the other three directions—east, west, and south. Early compasses were used as a backup for cloudy nights, when the North Star could not be seen. If you are lost on a clear night, you, too, can figure out the directions by locating the North Star.

How can the North Star stay in one place while all the other stars move across the sky? This may be easier to understand if you act out being the earth turning on its axis. Do this indoors, standing in the middle of a large room, such as a gym. Spin in one place and look at the walls. Everything is a spinning blur. Now look at the ceiling directly above you. That point seems to stay still. It is

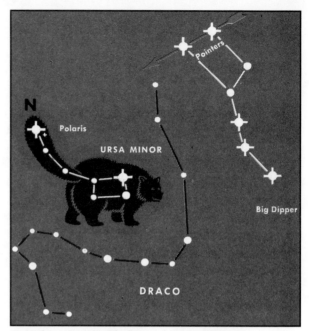

Polaris—the North Star—is the end of Ursa Minor's (Little Bear's) tail. It also begins the handle of the Little Dipper.

always visible no matter which wall you face. This is similar to standing on Earth and looking up at the North Star. The North Star is so far away that it is visible from any place north of the equator and is always in the same location.

Polaris has not always been the North Star, and will not always be. Earth slowly wobbles as it spins, coming back to the same position every 26,000 years. About 26,000 years ago, some other star was above the North Pole. In the future, around 13,000 years from now, the star Vega will be above the North Pole. Then it will be the North Star, and Polaris will be just another star in the sky.

Northwest Passage

The Northwest Passage is a sea route that connects the Atlantic and the Pacific oceans. It is about 900 miles (1,440 kilometers) long and passes by the North American coast of the Arctic Ocean. It is named "northwest" because, to Europeans, it lies to the north and west.

Ice and extreme cold prevent the Northwest Passage from being a practical route. Yet the passage has played an important part in North American history. While looking for such a passage, European explorers made many discoveries and claimed land in North America for their governments.

The search for a northwest passage began in the late 1400s. European traders wanted to find a shortcut to Asia. At that time, a voyage to Asia meant sailing around Africa and India, which took a long time. Traders thought sailing west across the Atlantic Ocean would be faster. After the voyages of Christopher Columbus, they realized that the Americas blocked the way. If only there were a water route through the continents!

While searching in the North for a northwest passage, John Cabot found Newfoundland in 1497. Since Cabot sailed under the English flag, he claimed parts of eastern Canada for England. In 1535, Jacques Cartier, too, was looking for a route to Asia. He sailed up the St. Lawrence River and claimed parts of Canada for France. (*See* **Cabot, John** and **Cartier, Jacques.**)

When Henry Hudson sailed up the Hudson River in 1609, he thought he had discovered the northwest passage. The next year, he made another voyage. This time, he was sure he had found the way. Instead, he had sailed through Hudson Strait into Hudson Bay. (*See* **Hudson, Henry.**)

As time went on, people realized they could travel from the Atlantic to the Pacific by sailing south down the coast of South America and then around its tip. Another way was to sail west to Central America and then cross the country of Panama on foot. The search for a northwest passage continued, but it was mainly to satisfy scientific curiosity.

Roald Amundsen of Norway was the first person to make a successful voyage through the Northwest Passage. The trip took Amundsen and his crew three years, from 1903 to 1906. The explorers faced danger from fog, huge icebergs, and blizzards. In 1944, a ship traveled through the Northwest Passage in a single season. It was commanded by a Canadian, Henry Larsen. (*See* **Amundsen, Roald.**)

Amundsen was the first to find the Northwest Passage (right). He sailed through it in 1906 in the ship *Gjöa* (below).

Northwest Territories

Capital: Yellowknife
Area: 1,322,900 square miles (3,426,311 square kilometers)
Population (1981): 45,741 (1985): about 50,500
Became a territory: June 23, 1870

The Northwest Territories is a vast, rugged area that stretches across northern Canada. It makes up about one-third of Canada's land, but only one out of 100 Canadians lives in this harsh region.

Land The Northwest Territories lies north of Canada's provinces. It is bordered by the Yukon Territory in the west and Hudson Bay in the east. It includes islands in the Arctic Ocean north of the mainland and in Hudson and James bays. The Mackenzie Mountains form the western boundary of the Northwest Territories. Directly east of the mountains is the Mackenzie River, the longest river in Canada. Waters from two of Canada's largest lakes—Great Slave Lake and Great Bear Lake—flow into the Mackenzie River. Most of the rest of the Northwest Territories is called the "barrens," because only small bushes and flowering plants can grow there.

History Norsemen from Greenland explored Baffin Island in the Northwest Territories around the year 1000. Beginning in the late 1500s, Europeans sailed around the Arctic islands and Hudson Bay. They were looking for a northwest passage, a water route between the Atlantic and Pacific oceans. (*See* **Northwest Passage.**)

Traders began to explore the Northwest Territories during the 1770s. Many worked for the Hudson's Bay Company, a trading business that owned the eastern part of the Northwest Territories. In 1870, the Hudson's Bay Company sold this area to the new nation of Canada.

For hundreds of years, the fur trade was the main source of income for the people of

Bush planes are an important means of travel in the huge, cold Northwest Territories.

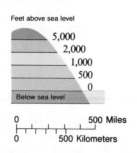

Feet above sea level

5,000
2,000
1,000
500
0
Below sea level

0 — 500 Miles
0 — 500 Kilometers

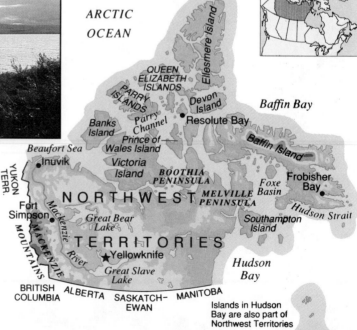

ARCTIC OCEAN

QUEEN ELIZABETH ISLANDS
PARRY ISLANDS
Ellesmere Island
Devon Island
Baffin Bay
Banks Island
Parry Channel
Resolute Bay
Prince of Wales Island
Baffin Island
Beaufort Sea
Victoria Island
Inuvik
BOOTHIA PENINSULA
Foxe Basin
Frobisher Bay
YUKON TERR.
NORTHWEST
MELVILLE PENINSULA
Hudson Strait
Fort Simpson
Great Bear Lake
Southampton Island
MACKENZIE MOUNTAINS
Mackenzie River
TERRITORIES
★Yellowknife
Hudson Bay
Great Slave Lake
BRITISH COLUMBIA
ALBERTA
SASKATCH-EWAN
MANITOBA

Islands in Hudson Bay are also part of Northwest Territories

the Northwest Territories. Today, the mining of zinc, gold, and petroleum is the most important activity.

People More than half of the people in the Northwest Territories are Eskimo or Indians. The rest are whites and *métis*—people of mixed white and Indian ancestry. The people work mostly as miners, traders, missionaries, or for the government. The largest town in the territory is the capital, Yellowknife, on Great Slave Lake.

Norway, *see* Scandinavia; Europe

Nova Scotia

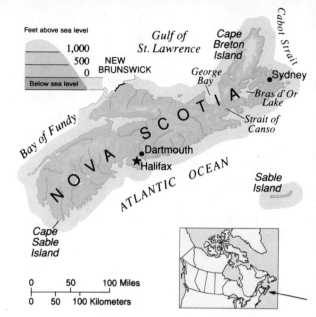

Capital: Halifax
Area: 21,420 square miles (55,478 square kilometers) (9th-largest province)
Population (1981): 847,442 (1985): about 878,300 (7th-largest province)
Became a province: July 1, 1867 (one of four original provinces)

Nova Scotia is one of Canada's four Atlantic Provinces. New Brunswick, Prince Edward Island, and Newfoundland are the others. Nova Scotia includes Cape Breton Island and part of mainland Canada. A short, narrow strip of land—the Isthmus of Chignecto—connects Nova Scotia's western border with New Brunswick. The isthmus keeps Nova Scotia from being completely surrounded by water—the Atlantic Ocean, the Bay of Fundy, and the Gulf of St. Lawrence.

Land No part of Nova Scotia is more than 60 miles (97 kilometers) from the sea. Warm ocean currents keep winters from being bitterly cold, and sea breezes make summers mild. Low, rolling hills line the northern shores of Nova Scotia. Rich farmlands lie inland. People raise apples, hay, and dairy cattle. Logs cut from the province's thick forests are used to make furniture, boats, and paper. Minerals found in Nova Scotia include coal, salt, and gypsum. Most coal mining is done on Cape Breton Island.

History The Micmac Indians were living in what is now Nova Scotia before the first Europeans arrived in the early 1500s. The French founded the colony of Port Royal in 1605. They called the area Acadia. France and Britain fought for control of Acadia for over 100 years. In 1621, King James I of Great Britain gave the area to Sir William Alexander of Scotland. Alexander named the land Nova Scotia—Latin for "New Scotland." France was forced to give Nova Scotia to the British in 1713.

The British distrusted the French Acadians and forced them to leave their lands in

A scenic highway follows the shoreline of Cape Breton Island.

1755. Some moved south to Louisiana. Some scattered to remoter parts of Canada. After a while, many returned to Acadia. But the hardships they endured in their wanderings are told in many poems and legends.

In the 1780s, after the American Revolution, many American colonists loyal to Britain moved to Nova Scotia. Fishing and shipbuilding helped the area grow rapidly during the 1800s. In 1867, Nova Scotia joined New Brunswick, Ontario, and Quebec to form the Dominion of Canada.

People Most settlements in Nova Scotia are on the coast or along inland river valleys. Close to shore, fishermen catch lobsters, herring, mackerel, and swordfish. Some go farther out in search of cod, haddock, and halibut. Halifax is the capital of Nova Scotia and the largest urban area in the Atlantic Provinces. Oil refining and the processing of food and fish are major activities.

novel, *see* literature

nuclear power

Nuclear power is one kind of energy we use to make electricity. We also use it to run submarines, ships, and space satellites.

Nuclear energy is different from the other kinds of energy we use every day. Almost all other energy comes either from the sun or from burning something. We burn oil or coal to make electricity and heat buildings. We burn gasoline to run cars and airplanes. We get energy to move our bodies from "burning" some of the foods we eat.

Nuclear power does not come from the sun or from burning something. It comes from breaking or splitting *atoms,* the tiny building blocks of all things. Atoms are so small that they can be seen only under the most powerful microscopes. (*See* **atom.**)

In the middle of each atom is the part called the *nucleus.* The nucleus is held together by tremendous forces. Usually, atoms are almost impossible to break apart. But

scientists have learned how to split the nuclei of some atoms and release their huge energy. Breaking an atom's nucleus to release energy is called *nuclear fission.*

The first atoms split by scientists were atoms of uranium, a rare metal. When uranium atoms break apart, pieces fly in all directions. Some of the pieces hit the nuclei of other uranium atoms and break them apart. These atoms release more energy and more flying pieces. This is called a *chain reaction.* If a chain reaction is not controlled, it will cause a great explosion.

Scientists first learned about nuclear energy in the 1930s. The first controlled chain reaction took place in Chicago, in 1944. The scientists were hoping to create an atomic bomb. The United States was fighting in World War II and wanted a powerful new weapon to help win the war. An atomic bomb was tested in 1945. A few months later, two bombs were dropped on Japanese cities. (*See* **nuclear weapon.**)

After World War II, scientists learned how to control nuclear chain reactions so that they could produce energy for other uses. Soon people began building nuclear *reactors* —huge plants where controlled nuclear reactions released energy that could be turned into electricity.

In many ways, a nuclear power plant is like any other power plant. In most power plants, heat from burning oil or coal turns water into steam. In a nuclear power plant, the heat from the nuclear chain reaction changes water into steam. The steam then turns huge generators to make electrical power. There are nuclear power plants in every region of the United States and in many other countries. (*See* **electric power.**)

People once hoped that nuclear power would someday be used to make almost all electricity. They thought it would be less expensive than oil or coal and would not send smoke and soot into the air. But nuclear power is not as cheap as we thought it would be. It also has many more dangers than we expected.

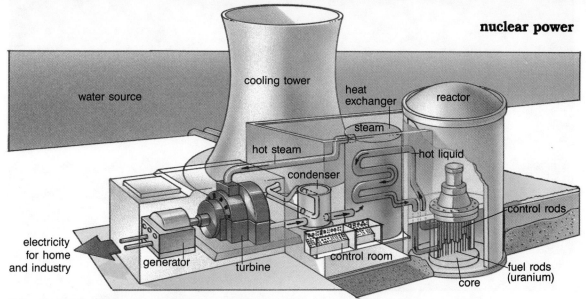

cooling tower

water source

heat exchanger

reactor

steam

hot steam

hot liquid

condenser

control rods

electricity for home and industry

generator

turbine

control room

core

fuel rods (uranium)

In a nuclear power plant, nuclear reactions in the reactor heat water to steam. The steam is used to turn a turbine and make electricity.

If something goes wrong at a nuclear power plant, people can lose control of the nuclear chain reaction. Then the nuclear reactor may send dangerous materials into the air and into the earth near the reactor. These materials are *radioactive*—they send out harmful particles and rays that can injure or kill plants and animals (including people).

Warning signs remind workers that nuclear materials are dangerous.

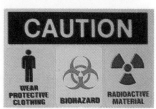

There have been several serious accidents at nuclear plants. In 1979, a reactor broke down at Three Mile Island in Pennsylvania. All the people around the plant were sent away from their homes. In 1986, a much more serious accident at Chernobyl in the Soviet Union killed more than 30 people. Thousands of others were made ill, and radioactive wastes were carried thousands of miles by the wind.

Nuclear power plants also produce solid radioactive wastes. These wastes are very dangerous, and we still do not know how to get rid of them safely. If they get into the air or water, they can poison living things. Most radioactive wastes are buried far from places where people live.

Nuclear power plants are also used to provide power for submarines and a few large ships. The U.S. Navy's nuclear submarines can stay underwater for weeks. One early atomic submarine, the *Nautilus,* was the first to carry humans under the polar ice cap to the North Pole.

Space scientists have learned to use very small nuclear generators in unmanned satellites and space probes. These tiny nuclear "factories" provide a small amount of electricity to help run the satellites. They can keep producing power for hundreds of years, using a tiny piece of "fuel." Since the unmanned vehicles are far away from living things, their radioactivity is not dangerous.

Scientists are trying to make nuclear energy safer and to find safe ways to get rid of radioactive wastes. Plans for new nuclear plants in the United States have been put off until we can be surer of their safety.

A nuclear-powered submarine comes to the ocean surface.

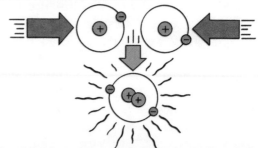

A nuclear explosion (above) gets its
huge force from *fission*—a reaction in
which atoms are broken apart (left).

nuclear weapon

Everything is made up of tiny atoms. They
are so small that they can be seen only
through the strongest microscopes. The center of an atom is called its *nucleus.* Powerful
forces hold the nucleus together. When the
nucleus is broken or when two nuclei are
forced to unite, tremendous energy is released. Nuclear weapons use this energy to
produce terrible explosions. (*See* **atom.**)

Nuclear weapons are exploded underground, above ground, underwater, or in the
air. They may be dropped as bombs from airplanes or be part of a missile. (*See* **missile.**)

There are two kinds of nuclear weapons
—atomic weapons and hydrogen weapons.
An atomic weapon uses *nuclear fission*—the
splitting of atoms. It uses atoms of either
uranium or plutonium. Both of these elements have large atoms. When these atoms
split, the power released is so great that it
causes nearby atoms to split, too. The splitting of one atom after another is called a

chain reaction. The chain reaction quickly
goes through an entire chunk of uranium or
plutonium, causing a tremendous explosion.

The first atomic weapon was exploded by
the United States on July 16, 1945, in New
Mexico. This bomb produced an explosion
equal to 20 kilotons (20,000 tons) of the
powerful explosive TNT. On August 6, 1945,
the United States dropped an atomic bomb
on Hiroshima, Japan. At that time, the
United States and Japan had been at war for
four years. Three days later, an atomic bomb
was dropped on Nagasaki, Japan. Japan
soon gave up the war. These were the only
two nuclear weapons used in war. (*See*
World War II.)

A hydrogen bomb, or H-bomb, is an example of a hydrogen weapon. Its explosion is

In the sun and other stars, energy
is produced by *fusion*—the joining
of two atoms to make one.

caused by *nuclear fusion.* Instead of splitting one atom apart, two atoms join together. When the atoms come together—in this case, hydrogen atoms—energy is released.

Hydrogen bombs are much more powerful than atomic bombs. A hydrogen bomb is set off in stages. First, an atomic bomb is exploded. The extreme heat then causes fusion of the hydrogen atoms, creating helium atoms and releasing even more energy.

Nuclear explosions cause terrific damage. The blast creates shock waves that knock down everything near the explosion. The blast also produces tremendous heat, causing fires for miles around.

A nuclear explosion also produces *radiation*—radioactive particles that kill or injure living things. People miles from the blast get radiation sickness and soon die.

Many radioactive particles are carried high into the atmosphere. Gradually, they settle back to the earth. This radioactive *fallout* can injure living things hundreds or thousands of miles from the blast.

---

number

A number tells how many things there are in a collection. Many children learn the names of the numbers and how to count even before they start school.

Early Numbers Ancient people used numbers to count things such as crops and animals. They counted on their fingers. Hand movements and sounds sometimes stood for numbers. They also counted by gathering objects—such as pebbles or sticks—or by scratching marks. One object or scratch stood for one item. But large numbers were not easy to show this way.

When people first began to use names for numbers, they named only very small numbers—one, two, and perhaps three. Sometimes, different number words are used for counting different things. For example, two socks are a *pair,* two musicians are a *duo,* and hunters call two shot birds a *brace.* For larger amounts, words such as *much, many, heaps,* or *piles* were good enough, even though they did not say exactly how many. Today, we say *millions* when we mean a large amount.

It is easy to understand how some number names came about. In Chinese, the word for *two* is the same as the word for *ears*—because people have two ears. Other languages use words for *eyes* or *wings* when they mean *two.*

Number Systems People needed to find a way to count larger groups of things, and they wanted to be exact. They needed a number system.

The numbers 1, 2, 3, 4, 5, 6, and so on are *counting numbers.* This is the first number system you learn. When you start at 1 and say the numbers in order, you are counting. There are other kinds of numbers besides these.

Zero is an important number. It can mean *none,* or *not any.* It can also be a point on a scale, such as a thermometer. If the temperature is 0°, that does not mean there is no temperature. It means the temperature measures to the point zero on the scale.

Below zero, and less in value, is another group of numbers. They are called *negative numbers.* They are −1, −2, −3, and so on. The counting numbers, zero, and the negative numbers form a group of numbers called *whole numbers.*

A number line helps to explain kinds of numbers. Whole numbers can be positive (above zero) or negative (below zero). A mixed number is between two whole numbers.

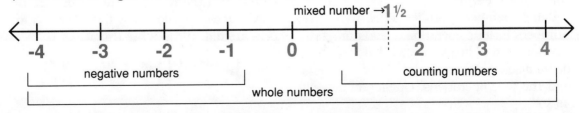

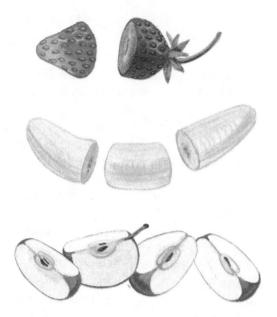

A fraction is a part—a half of a strawberry, a third of a banana, a fourth of an apple.

Numbers that name parts of things are called *fractions*. We use fractions such as one-half and one-quarter every day. When you use a whole number and a fraction, such as 4½, it is called a *mixed number*. (*See* **fraction.**)

A decimal is a special kind of fraction that measures in tenths or one hundredths. Our money system uses decimals. The amount $3.65 means 3 dollars and 65 one-hundredths of a dollar. (*See* **decimal.**)

Over the years mathematicians have discovered still other kinds of numbers. One kind is called *irrational.* These numbers cannot be written as whole numbers or as fractions. One such number is represented by the symbol π and is called *pi* (PIE). This number is used to measure circles. The symbol π stands for a value expressed as a decimal, of about 0.314. A computer has calculated the value of π as a decimal number to millions of places. But the answer never comes out even.

Using Numbers Students learn to use numbers in four operations—addition, subtraction, multiplication, and division. Students also learn basic rules about numbers and the four operations. Outside of school,

we use numbers often. When we tell the time, check the date, follow a recipe, or read a map, we use numbers. Teachers, carpenters, pilots, and policemen all use numbers in their work.

Learning to use numbers, and name them, took early people thousands of years. Once they had a system of numbers, it was easier for them to work together and to describe the world around them. But thousands of years passed before people began to write numbers. Written marks and symbols that stand for numbers are called *numerals.*

See also **arithmetic; mathematics;** and **numeral.**

numeral

A numeral is a mark or symbol that stands for a number. It is not the same as a number. If you study other civilizations, you may see different numerals. Numerals can vary, but numbers do not change. Even if you know more than one way to write the number five, the value or idea of five stays the same.

Early Numerals Early people used numbers for a long time before they began writing them. The first written numbers were probably scratches on the ground or marks on a stick. In fact, some early numeral systems use straight lines and probably came from these early marks. A farmer with six sheep might make a scratch to stand for each one, like this:

⑴⑴⑴

Lines that stand for single objects are called *tally marks.* You have probably used tally marks to keep score in a game. People usually make four tally marks and cross them with a fifth mark. When they count up the tally marks, they count by fives. Large numbers are difficult to write this way.

$$\text{卌 卌 ll} = 12$$

Symbols for the number three:
1. cave painting—three arrows in a horse
2. ancient Greek three
3. early Arabic three
4. American Indian date—October third
5. early Sumerian hieroglyph for three oxen
6. early Egyptian numeral one hundred three
7. Roman numeral III cut in stone
8. Inca *quipu*—knot-numeral—for three

Picture writing is another way of writing numbers. Some early people drew small figures or pictures to record numbers. A small picture of a boat might stand for a single boat, or it might mean more than one boat. Sometimes, drawings of different kinds of boats showed different amounts. Figures nearby might show how many people were in a boat. Some American Indian tribes used picture writing to record numbers until recent times.

In ancient Babylonia, people began to write on clay tablets. They wrote by pressing a wedge-shaped writing tool into the clay. Their system of writing is called *cuneiform* —from Latin words meaning "wedge-shaped." By changing the directions of the marks, and by arranging the marks into groups, the Babylonians were able to write all of the numerals they needed.

Early Egyptians used straight lines to write their numerals from one to ten. For example, the symbol for one was **|** and the symbol for three was **| | |**. The lines were arranged in special ways to make them easy to read. Other marks stood for larger numbers. For example, a coil was the numeral for one hundred, and a lotus flower meant one thousand.

The ancient Greeks used the letters of their alphabet as numerals. The first letter stood for one, the second letter meant two.

A small mark after a letter meant that it was being used as a numeral.

Roman numerals are still used in some places. Many children learn to use them in school. The numerals I, II, and III stand for the numbers one, two, and three. Letters, such as V, X, L, and C, take the place of five, ten, fifty, and one hundred. The numeral VI means five plus one—six. If the numeral for one—I—is in front of the larger number, it means subtract instead of add. So IV means five minus one—four. You have probably seen Roman numerals on clocks. The Romans were very powerful, so their system of numerals spread to many parts of the world. It was used in Europe until a new system came along.

Hindu-Arabic Numerals The system we use today is called the Hindu-Arabic system. This system started in India and was brought to Europe by Arabs. Europeans were using Roman numerals at the time. They soon saw that the Hindu-Arabic system was easier. There are ten numerals for the ten digits—0, 1, 2, 3, 4, 5, 6, 7, 8, and 9. (The word *digit* is Latin for "finger.") It is called a *decimal* system because it is based on the number ten. (The word *decimal* comes from the Latin word for "ten.")

The Hindu-Arabic numeral system is based on the number ten in more ways than one. We count to ten, then to ten tens (100), then to ten hundreds (1,000), and so on. This is probably because people once counted on their fingers or their toes. Names of numbers higher than ten come from the names of the digits. *Nineteen* means "nine and ten." *Thirty-seven* means "three tens and seven."

The Hindu-Arabic system has a symbol for zero. Today, we realize how important zero—0—is when we are writing numerals. After all, 7 is different from 70—or 7,000! Other numeral systems sometimes left a space to mean zero. Using a space for zero, 4 6 would be the numeral for four hundred six. It is harder to read than 406.

Today, most people in the world use Hindu-Arabic numerals. This makes it possible for people in different countries to trade, travel, and work together more easily.

It is possible to have a system based on something other than ten. The ancient Babylonian numerals were based on sixty. The Maya used a system based on twenty. Your computer is based on two.

BINARY NUMBERS

Our everyday number system is a *decimal* system — based on 10. Other number systems are based on other numbers. One system, the binary system, is based on the number 2. This system is used by computers. In the binary system, there are only two symbols or *numerals*. We can use the numerals **1** and **0**. Below are the counting numbers in binary:

Binary	Decimal	Binary	Decimal
1	1	1001	9
10	2	1010	10
11	3	1011	11
100	4	1100	12
101	5	1101	13
110	6	1110	14
111	7	1111	15
1000	8	10000	16

The right-hand place stands for 1's, and the next place is for 2's. Moving to the left, the next places are for 4's, 8's, and 16's.

To translate the decimal number 14 into binary, you need to find a combination of 8, 4, 2, and 1 that adds to 14. The answer is "one 8, one 4, one 2, and no 1's." So the binary form is **1110**.

There are only three addition facts and three subtraction facts in binary.

Addition	Subtraction
$0 + 0 = 0$	$0 - 0 = 0$
$1 + 0 = 1$	$1 - 0 = 1$
$1 + 1 = 10$	$1 - 1 = 0$

If you give a computer an arithmetic problem, it performs three steps:
1. It translates the decimal numbers you type into binary numbers.
2. It does the arithmetic in binary.
3. It translates the answer into decimal to show on the screen or printer.

If you give the computer this problem,	It translates into binary and does the arithmetic:	It translates the answer into decimal:
9 + 5	1001 + 101 1110	14

nursery rhyme, *see* Mother Goose

nut

Hazelnuts, walnuts, and chestnuts are three common kinds of nuts. Most people call peanuts, coconuts, and almonds nuts, too. But peanuts are related to peas and beans. Almonds, pistachios, cashews, and coconuts belong to the same group of fruits as peaches and plums. Scientists call these fruits *drupes*. (*See* **fruit** and **peanut**.)

A nut is a dry fruit that grows on certain trees. It has a hard outer shell and a softer inside part called a *kernel*. The kernel is the nut's seed. Each nut has only one kernel. A new nut tree sprouts from the kernel.

Nut-bearing trees and shrubs grow in many parts of the world. Many grow wild, and the nuts can be eaten as picked. But some acorns —the nuts of oak trees—taste bitter. The Indians of North America crushed acorns and then washed the acorn meal in water to remove the bitterness. They used the acorn meal in soups and other foods.

Nuts can be eaten alone or cooked with other foods, such as grains, vegetables, fruits, and meats. Nuts are rich in proteins and fats—two substances the body needs. Roasting nuts adds to their flavor. Cashews and almonds are ground into delicious "butters." Nuts are added to cakes, cookies, ice cream, pies, and candies. Marzipan is a soft candy made of ground almonds, sugar, and egg whites. In Spain, ground almonds are sweetened and then mixed with water to make a cool drink. Most nuts can be stored in their shells for months.

Walnut oil is used for cooking and as a polish for wood furniture. Almond oil is used in cosmetics. The wood of cherry, pecan, oak, and black walnut trees is used to make beautiful furniture. Parts of walnut trees and oak trees are boiled to make dyes for cloth. (*See* **hardwood tree**.)

Today, nut trees are planted on large farms. Nut growers raise almonds, pecans, walnuts, hazelnuts, and macadamia nuts, among others. Georgia and California are two of the leading nut-growing states in the United States. Hawaii is the world's top grower of macadamia nuts.

Most foods with shells are nuts, but some—such as peanuts and almonds—are not.
The walnuts on the tree (right) are smooth and green before they ripen.

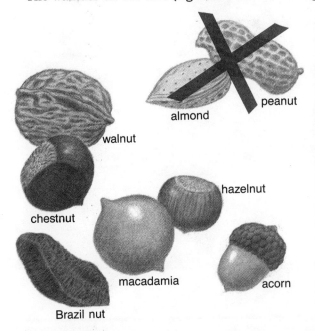

walnut
almond
peanut
chestnut
hazelnut
macadamia
acorn
Brazil nut

nutrition

Eating is an important part of our lives. Mealtimes can be the most enjoyable parts of the day. But the food we eat should do more than fill our stomachs. What we eat and drink should provide good nutrition if we are to grow properly and stay healthy.

Nutrition has several meanings. The study of food and how it affects health is called nutrition. Scientists who study nutrition are *nutritionists*. What people eat is also called nutrition. There can be "good nutrition" and "bad nutrition."

A Balanced Diet Nutritionists divide food into four groups—the *meat group,* the *bread group,* the *milk group,* and the *fruit-and-vegetable group.* A well-balanced meal should contain food from each of these groups. If you miss one group at one meal,

you can make it up at the next. But during each day, you should eat at least two servings from each group. If you do that, you have a *balanced diet.*

You do not always have to have milk, bread, and meat each day to have a balanced diet. Each food group has many foods in it. For example, the milk group includes yogurt, cheese, and butter.

The bread group includes cereals, such as corn flakes or oatmeal. It also includes pasta, such as macaroni, spaghetti, and noodles.

The meat group includes fish and chicken. It also includes some foods that are not meats at all—eggs, peanut butter, nuts, beans, and peas. These foods are in the meat group because they contain many of the same important substances as meat. People who do not eat meats can still get these substances by eating other foods in this group.

FOUR FOOD GROUPS

meat

bread

milk

fruits and vegetables

Spaghetti, one of the bread group, is good for providing energy.

Some foods are made from ingredients in several food groups. Pizza is a good example. Pizza dough is from the bread group. Tomato sauce is from the fruit-and-vegetable group. Cheese is from the milk group. Many toppings, such as sausage, are from the meat group. Eating pizza at every meal would not provide a balanced diet, though. To have a fully balanced diet, we need to eat many different foods from each food group.

Nutrients A balanced diet is important because it provides the many different *nutrients* your body needs. Nutrients are the particular substances that help the body grow and work properly. There are six groups of nutrients—proteins, fats, carbohydrates, vitamins, minerals, and water.

Protein is the main bodybuilder. It is important especially when you are growing, because your cells need protein to make more cells. Proteins are made from amino acids. Your body needs about 20 different amino acids. These amino acids are in protein foods. Foods in the meat, milk, and bread groups all have proteins. Those in the meat group are especially rich in this nutrient. (*See* **protein.**)

NUTRIENTS

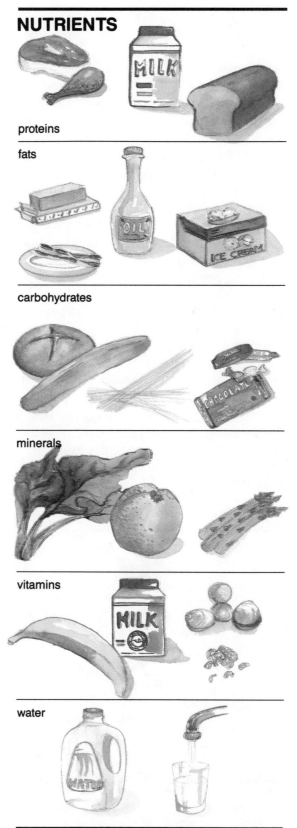

proteins

fats

carbohydrates

minerals

vitamins

water

Carbohydrates are foods that give you energy. The bread group is known for its carbohydrates. Runners may eat bowls of spaghetti the night before a race, because spaghetti keeps releasing energy for a long time. Other carbohydrates are found in sugar. Milk and fruits both have natural sugars. Candy and soft drinks have processed sugars. Sugars release energy for only a short time. (*See* **carbohydrate.**)

Fats can also provide energy, and they help to keep skin smooth and hair glossy. Milk and butter contain butterfat. Meats also contain fat. Other fat in our diets comes from oils that foods are cooked in. All fried foods, including potato chips and French fried potatoes, have oil in them. A little fat is important for good health. But most of us have too much fat in our diets. (*See* **fat.**)

Vitamins and minerals are needed in small amounts to keep the body running properly. If you do not get the vitamins and minerals you need, you may develop such conditions as poor eyesight, lack of energy, or poorly formed bones. Vitamins are found in each of the food groups. Some vitamins, such as vitamin C, are found only in fruits and vegetables. (*See* **vitamins and minerals.**)

Milk, fruit, and fruit juices provide important vitamins for good health.

Two important minerals are iron and calcium. Iron is necessary for the body to make red blood cells, which carry oxygen from the lungs to the rest of the body. There is iron in many vegetables and in liver. Calcium is used in building bones and teeth, and it helps regulate the activity of every cell in the body. Foods in the milk group are the main source of calcium.

Another important nutrient is water. People can live for weeks without food, but without water a person can die in two or three days. In blood, water helps to carry nutrients, antibodies, waste products, and other essentials to and from every part of the body. It bathes all the cells, and it moistens areas around the joints and mucous membranes. In saliva, water helps to make food in the mouth soft and easy to swallow. As sweat, water helps to prevent a buildup of heat inside the body. The kidneys use water to make urine, which carries wastes out of the body.

The average person needs to drink at least two quarts of liquids each day. If you exercise or sweat a lot, you need more. Part of the liquid should be water. But juices, milk, and fruits such as apples or oranges are also made up mostly of water.

In some parts of the world, people suffer from *malnutrition.* This means that they have serious health problems because they do not have enough to eat. People may also have health problems because they eat too much of certain kinds of foods. Doctors have learned that eating too much fat can contribute to heart disease and some forms of cancer. Other health problems may be caused by eating too much salt or sugar. Even some vitamins can be harmful if taken in large amounts.

Most of us think eating is fun. But we also need to pay attention to what we eat, and eat foods that are good for us. The food we eat gives us the nutrients our bodies need to stay in good shape. A balanced diet is an important part of staying healthy.

See also **food.**

The letter *O* began with this ancient Egyptian symbol that looked like an eye.

The Semites borrowed the Egyptian symbol. They called it *'ayin*, their word for "eye."

The Phoenicians were the first to draw the symbol as a simple circle, around 1000 B.C.

Oakley, Annie

Annie Oakley was a popular performer in Buffalo Bill's Wild West Show during the late 1800s. Oakley's keen eye and steady aim with a gun made her a world-famous *sharpshooter*—a person who can hit a target with amazing accuracy.

Oakley was born in Ohio, in 1860. One of eight children, she was named Phoebe Anne Oakley Mosee. Her parents were poor. Her father died when she was four. The family

In her day, Annie Oakley was a better shot than almost anyone else, man or woman.

struggled, and often had little to eat. One day, when she was about nine, Oakley took her father's shotgun and went into the forest. She killed a running quail with her very first shot. After that, she earned money shooting game animals for sale.

At the age of 15, Oakley won a shooting contest against a famous marksman named Frank E. Butler. Within a year, the two were married and began to perform as a sharpshooting act with circuses. Taking the name Annie Oakley, the short, slim young woman soon became an audience favorite. She joined Buffalo Bill's show as a trick shooter in 1885, and starred in it for 17 years. Oakley amazed audiences by shooting dimes thrown into the air. She could hit a playing card held with the thin edge toward her from 30 yards (27 meters) away. Oakley died in 1926.

See also **Buffalo Bill.**

observatory

An observatory is a place where astronomers study stars, planets, and other heavenly bodies. It usually has a telescope and other equipment.

An *optical observatory* has a domeshaped roof with *shutters* in the roof that open to let the telescope point skyward. Many of these telescopes collect pictures on film or videotape. Astronomers also study the heavens for things that are not visible, such as radio waves. For this, they need a *radio observatory*, where there is a *radio telescope*. A radio telescope is a big, dish-shaped *reflector* that focuses radio waves onto an antenna. Both kinds of observatories use computers to guide the telescopes.

Ancient peoples had observatories that helped them follow the movements of the sun, moon, and stars. Stonehenge, an ancient circle of standing stones in England, was probably built to predict the seasons. In ancient Egypt and Mesopotamia, observatories were set up in temples. People used them to figure out when to have religious festivals and when to plant and harvest crops. The Maya in Central America and the Anasazi in North America built observatories. The Maya made a complicated calendar

Observatories like this one in Arizona help us study the stars and planets.

based on their observations. (*See* **Stonehenge** and **Maya.**)

These early observatories were often an arrangement of markers or slits. Their positions lined up with the rising or setting of the sun, moon, planets, or stars at certain times of the year. For example, they might mark the *summer solstice*—when the sun rises at its most northern point. The observer always looked at the markers or slits from the same position.

The telescope was invented by a Dutchman in the early 1600s. The Italian astronomer Galileo built one for himself in 1609, and used it to make important discoveries about the heavens. The telescope was soon being used in all observatories. With it, astronomers could look deeper into space and learn more about the movements of heavenly bodies. (*See* **Galileo.**)

Over the years, telescopes have grown larger and more complicated, and so have the observatories that house them. The Mount Palomar observatory, in California, built in 1948, is a towering, round structure that houses a 200-inch (5-meter) telescope. Machines open the large shutter in the domed roof. Machines also turn the entire dome, so that as the earth rotates, the telescope stays pointed where the astronomer wants it. For many years, Mount Palomar's telescope was the biggest, most powerful telescope in the world. Today, observatories are being planned or built to house even larger ones and equip them with the most up-to-date computer controls.

Observing the heavens from Earth is not easy. The atmosphere, especially when it is polluted, keeps observers from seeing clearly. Lights from cities make it hard for telescopes to pick up faint lights. The machinery jiggles the telescopes and creates heat that makes observing difficult. Radio interference from cities and towns is a problem for radio telescopes.

Radio observatories are usually built in valleys, where surrounding mountains block interference. Optical observatories are built on mountaintops, far from cities. Astronomers choose mountaintops because the earth's atmosphere is thinner and cleaner there. Several new observatories have been built on top of Mauna Kea, an extinct volcano in Hawaii. Mauna Kea is about 4,200 meters (14,000 feet) high—above four-tenths of Earth's atmosphere.

Scientists are trying to get past Earth's atmosphere in another way—by launching space satellites that do some of the work of observatories. The U.S. *Project Skylab* space station was in orbit around Earth from 1973 to 1979. It was visited by three teams of astronauts and gave us clearer pictures of the sun than we had ever had before. Russia's space stations *Salyut* and *Mir* have done similar work. But a lasting space observatory is still in the future.

See also **astronomy; radio telescope;** and **telescope.**

ocean

Oceans are the wide, deep bodies of salty water that cover three-fourths of Earth. People have always been fascinated by the oceans. An ocean is beautiful, and it is changing all the time. The ocean appeals to our imaginations because it suggests great power and endless possibilities. We are amazed by mighty ocean storms, yet we feel reassured by the day-in, day-out rhythm of the tides. The world's highest mountain and deepest gorge are found on the ocean floor. The ocean is very familiar and very mysterious at the same time.

Islands and continents interrupt the ocean, rising above sea level. The continents are made of the lighter rocks of the earth's crust. The crust surrounding the continents is made of heavier rocks. These rocks form the bottom of large, bowl-shaped hollows in the ocean floor called *ocean basins*. The ocean basins are about 4 or 5 kilometers (2½ or 3 miles) below sea level.

We sometimes think of Earth's oceans as one continuous world ocean, with the Pacific, Atlantic, Indian, and Arctic oceans as its parts. Some people call the waters around Antarctica the Antarctic Ocean. But most people consider those waters to be parts of the Pacific, Atlantic, and Indian oceans.

The Pacific, the largest ocean, covers 166 million square kilometers (64 million square miles). This is a greater area than that covered by all of the continents. The Arctic Ocean, the smallest, covers about 9 million square kilometers (3½ million square miles). It is about as large as the United States.

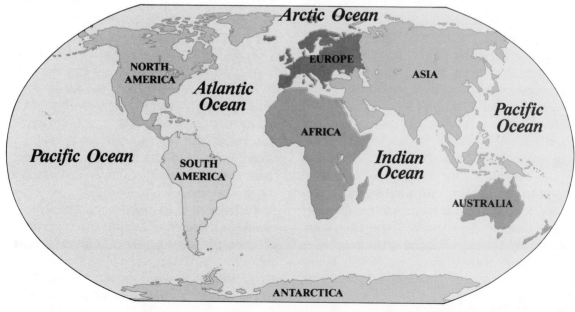

Origin of the Oceans When the earth first formed, over 4½ billion years ago, its surface was so hot that any water turned to water vapor. More water vapor came out of volcanoes. The water vapor hung suspended as clouds in the earth's new atmosphere. About 4 billion years ago, the earth's surface cooled below 100° C (212° F). Some of the water vapor turned to liquid and fell as rain. As water collected, the oceans began to form.

Water began to flow across the land in streams and rivers. As it flowed across the bare, jagged rocks, the water dissolved minerals from the rocks. These dissolved minerals are called *salts.*

Streams and rivers carried the salts to the low basins. When water evaporated from the new oceans to form clouds, the salts stayed behind. This is how the oceans and seas became salty and why they stay that way.

The Changing Oceans The earth's crust is divided into large plates. Ever since they formed, the plates have been slowly moving over the earth's surface. As they move, the oceans change size and shape. (*See* **continental drift.**)

The level of ocean water changes, too. At the height of the last ice age, much of the world's water was frozen into thick ice sheets. Sea level was more than 120 meters (400 feet) lower than it is now. The eastern shore of North America extended as much as 160 kilometers (100 miles) farther east than it does now. As the climate became warmer, the huge ice sheets melted, and the level of the oceans rose. (*See* **ice age.**)

Oceans and Weather The ocean has a strong influence on the earth's weather. The rain and snow that fall on land begin as water evaporating from the ocean. When seawater evaporates, the water vapor is carried up into the sky by warm, rising air. As it rises, it cools until it forms clouds of water vapor and tiny ice crystals. These clouds are blown by the winds until they pass over land. There, if their temperature falls below a certain point, they release their water as rain or snow.

Providing water for rain and snow is only one of the ways oceans influence climate and weather on land. Another way is the cooling caused by ocean winds. *Meteorologists*—scientists who study weather—call such winds *sea breezes.* They blow because of differences in temperature between areas of land and water.

On a clear, sunny day, the land heats up faster than does the ocean. In the morning, as land temperatures rise, the air over the land quickly becomes heated. Hot air is lighter than cold air, so it begins to rise. As it rises, cooler, heavier air from over the ocean flows in to take its place. This movement of cool ocean air from water to land is the sea breeze.

Sea breezes tend to keep the temperature along the coast from getting either very cold or very hot. Warm ocean currents affect coastal areas in the same way. Regions that are far inland tend to have very hot summers and very cold winters. (*See* **ocean current.**)

Oceans cover three-fourths of Earth's surface. Submersibles help us explore the unknown regions beneath the seas.

The ocean air blown inland by sea breezes in summer is not only cool, it is moist. In some parts of the world, you can actually see this moist ocean air come spilling over the land as coastal fog. Northern California receives only about 50 centimeters (20 inches) of rain each year—half of what New England gets. But its coast and forests stay green from the wet sea breezes that blow in every day from the Pacific.

Oceans and Life   Some scientists say that life on Earth began in the ocean, with bacteria and primitive, one-celled algae.

The ocean is full of living things. Animals live at all levels of the ocean, from the surface to the seafloor. The ocean is full of fish and mollusks. It is also home to some mammals, such as whales, dolphins, and porpoises. Among the reptiles, only sea turtles and sea snakes make their home in the salty ocean, and they come ashore to lay their eggs. Other animals, too, such as walrus and penguins, spend part of their lives in the ocean and part on the shore. Ocean plants, often called *seaweed,* live near the surface and in shallow water where sunlight can reach them. (*See* **fish; mammal; reptile;** and **ocean plants.**)

The ocean is important to people for many reasons. Most of the world's people live near an ocean or sea. Its plants and animals are rich sources of food for people. And since the beginning of human history, ocean waters have been highways for fishermen, travelers, traders, soldiers, and explorers.

In the last 100 years, people have begun to explore the ocean itself. *Oceanographers*—scientists who study the ocean—have learned a great deal about how the ocean behaves and about its resources. Oceanographers use such modern tools as sonar equipment and *submersibles*—undersea craft that are designed for exploring beneath the ocean surface. They have made some astonishing discoveries. They have learned how new ocean floor is created. They have discovered kinds of deepwater fish and other forms of sea life we never knew existed. Many of their discoveries have helped other scientists find out more about the nature of our planet.

Since the 1960s, we have learned that the seafloor contains valuable deposits of minerals, such as manganese and copper—and even gold and silver. It also contains vast amounts of fossil fuels, and people have built offshore wells to pump petroleum and gas from below the ocean floor.

See also **Arctic Ocean; Atlantic Ocean; Indian Ocean; Pacific Ocean; ocean floor; atmosphere; continent;** and **earth history.**

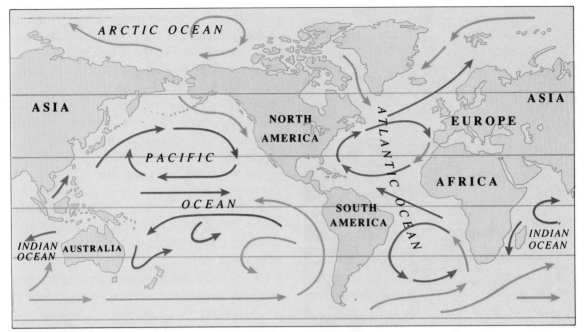

Currents north of the equator run in huge clockwise circles.
Currents south of the equator run counterclockwise.

ocean current

An ocean current is a flow of water in the ocean. There are two main kinds of ocean currents.

The ocean currents that sailors and fishermen learn about in their years at sea are caused by wind pushing on the surface water of the ocean. These currents are called *wind-driven* or *surface currents*.

The other kind of current moves only very deep water, 900 meters (3,000 feet) or more below the surface. These currents are caused by differences in the weight of water from one part of the ocean to another. Cold water tends to be heavier than warm water. The difference causes deep currents to flow from cold, polar areas toward the warmer areas of the equator. Water with more salt in it is also heavier than water with less salt. This also causes currents deep in the ocean.

In a wind-driven current, such as the Gulf Stream, water can move along as fast as 9 kilometers (5½ miles) per hour. But in deep currents, water moves much more slowly. Deep currents usually flow less than 30 meters (100 feet) per hour.

Wind-driven or surface currents affect only the upper layer of ocean water. This layer extends to a depth of not more than 90 meters (300 feet). These currents usually move in the same direction in which the winds are blowing.

Scientists have made maps of the world showing the direction in which the winds blow at different times in different places. These maps show that, year after year, winds blow in one direction in winter and another direction in summer. Scientists have also made maps of the world showing ocean currents. On these maps, you can see that currents change from one season to another, just as the winds change.

In some parts of the world, these changes are not very great. For example, in the North Atlantic Ocean, the Gulf Stream is a little farther from land in summer than in winter. In other parts of the world, currents go through great seasonal changes. A current in the Indian Ocean is one example. In winter, during India's dry season, this current flows west off the southern tip of the continent. In summer, when the winds blow in the opposite direction, bringing the heavy monsoon rains,

Where cold currents bring up food from deep in the sea, huge schools of fish gather to eat.

the current changes, too, and flows east. (*See* **Gulf Stream** and **wind.**)

Some currents carry warm waters from near the equator toward cold water near the North and South poles. The Gulf Stream is one such current. Another is the Kuroshio or Japan Current, a Pacific Ocean current. It flows from the Philippines north past Japan and then east across the North Pacific. Warm currents such as these help to warm the climates of the northern coasts.

Not all ocean currents are warm. In summer, along the West Coast of the United States, the south-flowing California current brings cold ocean water close to shore. It cools the air along the coast, causing wet, heavy fogs throughout the summer. This helps thick forests to grow in areas that would otherwise be dry and bare.

Another kind of cold current, called an *upwelling,* occurs along coasts where winds blow from north to south. There are upwellings along the west coast of Mexico and the coasts of Ecuador, Peru, and Chile. In these places, the north-south winds blow the surface water out toward the open ocean. When this happens, colder, deeper water flows in

to take its place. This flow of cold water brings with it things that fish like to eat. While the upwellings continue, large schools of fish are attracted to these areas.

Sometimes a flow of warm water comes south across the equator and keeps upwellings from happening along the coasts of Peru and Ecuador. This current is called El Niño—Spanish for "The Child"—because it usually occurs around Christmas, when the birth of Jesus Christ is celebrated.

When El Niño comes, the fish do not. In countries such as Peru that depend heavily on ocean fishing, fishermen lose millions of dollars. This is only one of the ways that El Niño causes trouble. The warming effect of the current—as much as 7° C (13° F)—causes faster evaporation of ocean water. This increased moisture in the air causes heavy rainfall and flooding in some parts of the world, and drought in others.

Ocean currents affect life on Earth. Many effects are good. The Gulf Stream and the Kuroshio make northern coastal climates milder in winter, while upwellings help fishermen catch fish.

See also **ocean** and **tide.**

ocean floor

If all the seas and oceans dried up or drained away, a strange world would appear. In the middle of the Pacific Ocean, you would see the world's tallest mountain—even taller than Mount Everest. You would also see deep gorges. One is the deepest place on Earth—11,033 meters (36,198 feet) below the earth's surface.

The ocean floor is a varied and active world, but it was almost completely unknown before this century. In the middle of the 1800s, a new invention—the telegraph—made it important to find out what the ocean floor looked like. Telegraph cables were being laid across the floor of the Atlantic Ocean, linking North America with Europe. Scientists and engineers began to make maps of the ocean floor.

At first, they measured the depth of the water by lowering a heavy weight until it reached the bottom. In the 1940s, they found another way to measure the ocean's depth. They bounced sound waves off the ocean floor and measured the time it took for the waves to return. They knew that the longer the time, the deeper the water.

A Trip Across the Bottom of a Sea Let's take an imaginary trip across the floor of the Atlantic Ocean. We'll start at the North American coast.

As we move out from the shore, the water gets gradually deeper. This part of the ocean floor is called the *continental shelf.* It is an underwater edge of the continent of North America. Most of the shelf is flat, but there are some long, steep gorges. These gorges, cut into the shelf by the water, are called *submarine canyons*—underwater canyons.

All continents have a continental shelf. The continental shelf is quite wide in some places. It extends 160 kilometers (100 miles) or more from the eastern shores of North and South America. In other places—such as off the west coast of the Americas—it is narrow or even absent.

As we travel out across the shelf, we finally reach a place where the ocean bottom slants much more steeply. This part of the ocean floor is called the *continental slope*. It starts at a depth of from 120 to 180 meters (400 to 600 feet). Here, the ocean floor begins to drop like the side of a broad mountain range, and the water quickly becomes very deep.

When we reach the bottom of the slope, we find ourselves on a broad plain that extends hundreds of miles ahead of us. The water here is over 5 kilometers (3 miles) deep. This plain is called an *ocean basin.* The ocean basin is of special interest to *geologists*—scientists who study the structure of the earth. It holds important clues to the mystery of *continental drift*—the slow

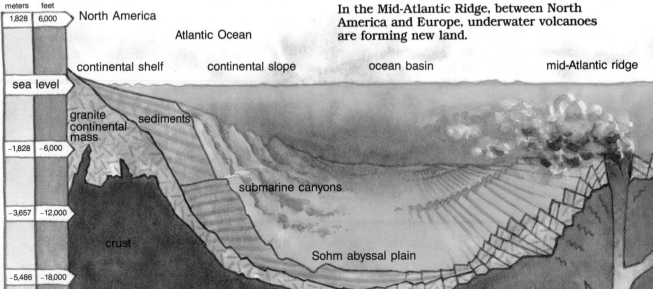

In the Mid-Atlantic Ridge, between North America and Europe, underwater volcanoes are forming new land.

meters	feet
1,828	6,000
sea level	
−1,828	−6,000
−3,657	−12,000
−5,486	−18,000

North America

Atlantic Ocean

continental shelf   continental slope   ocean basin   mid-Atlantic ridge

granite continental mass   sediments

submarine canyons

crust

Sohm abyssal plain

Near the ocean floor, there are strange-looking fish, such as the deep-sea angler (left). There are also many animals without backbones, such as the red tube worm (right).

movement of the continents across the surface of the earth. (*See* **continental drift**.)

As we cross the ocean basin, we see clusters and chains of mountains in the distance. These mountains are volcanoes. Some stopped erupting long ago, but some are still active. Many are clustered along the *Mid-Atlantic Ridge*. This underwater ridge stretches north and south for thousands of miles. It is just one branch of an underwater chain of volcanic mountains that is 64,000 kilometers (40,000 miles) long! The chain—called the *Mid-Oceanic Ridge*—completely encircles the earth.

Along the Mid-Oceanic Ridge, scientists have discovered geysers spouting hot water from deep inside the earth. Geysers, such as

"Old Faithful" in Yellowstone National Park, are easy to see on land. But underwater geysers were not found until 1979 in the Pacific, and the ones near the Mid-Atlantic portion of the Mid-Oceanic Ridge were found even more recently—in 1986. The hot water contains large amounts of minerals that harden when they hit the cold ocean water. They have formed mounds rich in iron, copper, gold, and silver near the geysers.

In the 1960s, geologists discovered that sections of the earth's crust on either side of the Mid-Oceanic Ridge are being pushed away from it. Lava erupting from the ridge is creating new crust. As new crust forms along the Mid-Oceanic Ridge, the seafloor spreads to make room for it. This pushes apart the *plates*—sections of crust—on each side of the ridge.

But the earth is a giant sphere. When you push apart the plates of its shell on one side of the world, they push against other plates elsewhere. When two plates collide, one slides under the other. *Submarine trenches* deep beneath the surface of the ocean are evidence of such collisions.

Submarine trenches are the very deepest places on the surface of the earth. Some reach down 10 to 11 kilometers (6 to 7 miles) below sea level. Geologists have discovered that these deep cracks in the ocean floor mark where one part of the earth's crust has collided with another.

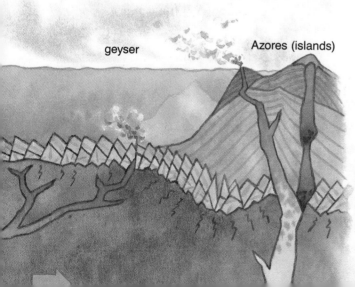

geyser Azores (islands)

ocean plants

Ocean plants include some of the many kinds of algae that live in oceans. Since ocean plants need sunlight to live, they are found near the surface and in shallow water. Ocean plants are also called *seaweeds*. Some are giant kelp that grow up to 60 meters (200 feet) long. Other algae are only a single cell. Still others look like land plants and grow in underwater forests.

Many of today's scientists do not think these living things should be called plants. Some scientists place all algae in the protist kingdom. Other scientists place the large algae in the plant kingdom and the one-celled algae in the protist kingdom. (*See* **protist**.)

Some of the most important algae in the oceans are the one-celled *diatoms* and *dinoflagellates*. They have tiny, glasslike shells around their cells. The shell of a diatom has a top and a bottom that fit over one another. Diatoms, unlike dinoflagellates, are among the masses of tiny, free-floating ocean plants and animals called *plankton*.

There are billions of ocean plants near the surface of the oceans. They are a major source of oxygen for all the living things on Earth. They are also important sources of food for the ocean's other living things—even those living in the deepest regions. Ocean plants serve as the producers in the ocean food chains. (*See* **food chain**.)

Dinoflagellates are important in another way. They produce poisons that can harm fish and other ocean animals. Sometimes dinoflagellates reproduce rapidly along a seacoast. They may turn the water red, causing what is called a *red tide*. Red tides kill hundreds of living things and make fish and shellfish unsafe to eat.

Other tiny algae can destroy fish and crustaceans by using up the oxygen in the water. The algae become so thick that they prevent sunlight from reaching lower levels. They also leave no space for other important food plants.

Flowering plants that we see on land do not grow in the oceans. Some of these grow near the shore, but they cannot grow completely submerged in salt water. Flowering plants such as mangroves and spartina must keep some parts out of the salt water at least part of the time.

See also **algae** and **kelp**.

A giant kelp (bottom) can stretch hundreds of feet. The tiny plants (right) can be seen only with a microscope.

The eight tentacles of an octopus (above) have suckers on their bottom surfaces. A squid (right) has ten arms and two fins. Octopuses and squid eat other animals.

octopuses and squid

Octopuses and squid are mollusks that live in all the oceans of the world. They are related to clams, oysters, and snails. Like all mollusks, they have soft bodies enclosed by a *mantle*—a fold of tissue. Unlike some mollusks, octopuses and squid do not have shells around their bodies. But scientists think that the ancestors of octopuses did have shells.

Octopuses and squid come in many sizes. Some squid are only 5 centimeters (2 inches) long. The giant squid is the world's largest *invertebrate*—animal without a backbone. It may be 18 meters (60 feet) long.

An octopus has eight arms, which are called *tentacles*. A squid has two fins at the tail end and ten arms. Only the two longest arms are called tentacles. Both animals have rows of suckers on their arms and tentacles. Octopuses and squid are *carnivores*—meat-eaters. They use their arms and tentacles to catch fish and other sea animals. The suckers hold the food while the arms carry it to the mouth. The mouth has a powerful beak, like the beak of a parrot. It is used to break shells and tear apart food.

Octopuses and squid swim by jet propulsion. They suck water into their soft, saclike bodies, and then shoot the water out. This causes them to move in the direction opposite the direction of the jet of water—often backward.

An octopus spends most of its time on the seafloor. It rests between rocks or in a sandy burrow, or slowly swims looking for prey—the animals it eats. An octopus would rather run from an enemy than fight. When frightened, the octopus releases a dark liquid from a special *ink sac*. The cloudy water confuses the enemy while the octopus hurries away. Most octopuses can also change color. When they are excited or want to hide, they may turn blue, brown, red, purple, white, or even striped!

Squid are excellent swimmers. One group—the *sea arrows* or *flying squid*—can swim so fast that they leap high out of the water. Like the octopuses, squid have ink sacs. But they are fierce creatures. A giant squid will even attack a small whale.

In many parts of the world, people catch octopuses and squid for food. Squid used for food are often called *calamari*.

See also **mollusk.**

Ohio

Capital: Columbus
Area: 41,330 square miles (107,045 square kilometers) (35th-largest state)
Population (1980): 10,797,603 (1985): about 10,744,000 (7th-largest state)
Became a state: March 1, 1803 (17th state)

Ohio is a rich manufacturing, agricultural, and mining state with a large population. It has played an important role in the life of the United States for almost 200 years.

Ohio is in the part of the north-central United States called the Midwest. Ohio is bordered by Michigan on the northwest and Indiana to the west. Pennsylvania and West Virginia are to the east. West Virginia and Kentucky are on the south. Lake Erie forms most of the northern boundary. The Ohio River curves around the eastern and southern borders. (*See* **Ohio River.**)

Land Western Ohio and the strip of land along Lake Erie are mostly flat or gently rolling. Eastern Ohio is hilly.

Many rivers flow through Ohio. The rivers made travel fairly easy for early explorers and fur traders, and later for settlers.

Ohio's soil and climate are good for agriculture. Corn and wheat grow well, and so do fruits and vegetables. Dairy farms and raising beef cattle, hogs, and sheep are also important to the state's economy.

Ohio is rich in natural resources. Coal has been mined in the southern part of the state since 1835. Petroleum and natural gas were discovered in Ohio soon after statehood. About one-tenth of the nation's salt comes from Ohio. It also ranks high in the production of stone, especially limestone and sandstone. Both of these are used for buildings and in manufacturing.

History About 1,000 years ago, prehistoric Indians called Mound Builders lived in Ohio. They heaped up earth and stones to make hills in which they buried their dead. Some of the hills were shaped like stars or snakes. Scientists are still studying the mounds to learn about the life of these ancient people.

France claimed the Ohio area because two Frenchmen—Jolliet and La Salle—were probably the first Europeans to see it. The region was also claimed by England. The dispute led to the French and Indian War between the French and British. The war ended in 1763 when France gave up its claim to the land. Indian uprisings followed the war, but settlers stayed. (*See* **Jolliet, Louis; La Salle, Sieur de;** and **French and Indian War.**)

After the American Revolution, the United States took control of the area. In 1787, Ohio became part of what was called the Northwest Territory. Marietta, the first permanent settlement in Ohio, was founded in 1788 to serve as the capital of the territory. Many men who had fought in the Revolution were given land in the area, and settlements sprang up quickly. The Indians were defeated in 1794. By 1803, there were so many people in Ohio that it was organized into a state.

People Industry developed early in Ohio, and immigrants from Europe swelled the population of the large industrial cities. Even now, more Ohioans make a living in manufacturing than in agriculture or mining.

Iron and steel are the principal industries. No state makes more machines and machine tools than Ohio. The state is also known for its tires and other rubber products.

Cleveland is the state's largest city and a major port on Lake Erie. Its factories manufacture heavy industrial machinery and many other products. Raw materials of all kinds are shipped to Cleveland. Columbus, in central Ohio, is the second-largest city and the state capital. It is a trade center for the farmlands that surround it. Cincinnati, the third-largest city, is a busy port on the Ohio River. It is a food-processing center, and jet engines are produced there.

Ohio is sometimes called the "mother of presidents," because seven United States presidents have come from the state. They are Ulysses S. Grant, Rutherford B. Hayes, James A. Garfield, Benjamin Harrison, William McKinley, William Howard Taft, and Warren G. Harding. (*See* **presidents of the United States.**)

There are many other well-known Ohioans. Astronauts John Glenn and Neil Armstrong are Ohio natives, as were inventors Thomas Alva Edison and Wilbur and Orville Wright. John Chapman ("Johnny Appleseed") wandered in central Ohio for many years, planting and tending his apple trees.

The skyline of Cleveland, Ohio, where the Cuyahoga River meets Lake Erie.

Scarlet carnation

ELEVATION   Feet

1000 — 1500
600 — 1000
300 — 600

0   MILES   30

Cardinal

MICHIGAN

Toledo

MUSEUM CONTAINING LIBRARY AND DOCUMENTS OF RUTHERFORD B. HAYES (19th president of the United States)   Fremont

Findlay

Lima

COMMODORE PERRY DEFEATS BRITISH IN BATTLE OF LAKE ERIE, 1813

Lake Erie

Sandusky   Oberlin   Elyria   Lorain

OBERLIN COLLEGE (world's first college to admit women, 1873)

Orange   Euclid

Cleveland Heights   Cleveland   Lakewood

Akron

"RUBBER CAPITAL OF THE U.S."

Mansfield   Canton

BIRTHPLACE OF JAMES GARFIELD (20th president of the U.S.)

PENNSYLVANIA

Warren   Niles   Youngstown

BIRTHPLACE OF WILLIAM McKINLEY (25th president of the U.S.)

TOMB OF WARREN HARDING (29th president of the U.S.)   Marion

O H I O

INDIANA

River

BIRTHPLACE OF BENJAMIN HARRISON (23rd president of the U.S.)   Springfield

Miami   Dayton

Middletown

Hamilton

BIRTHPLACE OF WILLIAM HOWARD TAFT (27th president of the U.S.)

★Columbus

Scioto River

Newark

Zanesville

Lancaster

Steubenville

WEST VIRGINIA

Muskingum River   Marietta

Ohio River

Chillicothe

Cincinnati

North Bend

TOMB OF WILLIAM H. HARRISON (9th president of the U.S.)

BIRHTPLACE OF ULYSSES S. GRANT (18th president of the U.S.)

Point Pleasant   Portsmouth

KENTUCKY

▲ Historical Sites and Points of Interest

Ohio River

The Ohio is one of North America's major rivers. It is 981 miles (1,579 kilometers) long and flows through the east-central part of the United States.

The Ohio River begins where the Allegheny and Monongahela rivers come together at Pittsburgh, Pennsylvania. It flows west through Pennsylvania, then southwest along the state borders of Ohio, West Virginia, Indiana, Kentucky, and Illinois. At Cairo, Illinois, it empties into the Mississippi River.

The Tennessee, Cumberland, and Wabash rivers are among the Ohio's *tributaries*. A tributary is a river that flows into a larger river. The Ohio itself is a tributary of the Mississippi River. It contributes more water to the Mississippi than does any other river. The Ohio River drains about 203,900 square miles (528,101 square kilometers) of land.

The Iroquois and Shawnee Indians lived along the Ohio in the 1600s. The word *ohio* means "bright," "shining," or "beautiful" in the Iroquois language. Sieur de La Salle, a French explorer, was probably the first European to see the great river. He may have found it in 1669. The British won control of the Ohio River Valley after the French and Indian War ended in 1763. Twenty years later, they surrendered the area to the United States. (*See* **French and Indian War** and **La Salle, Sieur de.**)

The Ohio River was an important trade route during the 1700s. Settlers heading west traveled along the river on their way to the Northwest Territory. This area of land was north of the Ohio River, west of Pennsylvania, and east of the Mississippi River.

In the past, melting snow or heavy rainstorms often made the Ohio River spill over its banks, causing terrible floods. In summer, water levels dropped so low that many boats could not travel on the river. Today, canals, locks, and dams control the flow of water along the river. Barges loaded with raw materials or finished products can use the river all year long. Coal, crude oil, gasoline, sand, iron, and steel are among the items carried by Ohio River barges. Major ports along the Ohio include Pittsburgh, Pennsylvania; Wheeling, West Virginia; Cincinnati, Ohio; and Louisville, Kentucky.

oil

There are many kinds of oil. Some kinds come from plants and animals. We use them for cooking and in cosmetics. Some can be burned as fuel for lamps. But usually we use the word *oil* to refer to *petroleum*.

Petroleum is oil that comes from the ground. It is used to make the world's most important fuels. Gasoline for cars comes from petroleum. So do diesel fuels for trucks and airplanes. Heating oil for homes, factories, and offices is also made from petroleum.

Where Oil Comes From Thousands of years ago, people in China scooped up small amounts of oil from the surface of the ground. They burned it for cooking and heating. It was not a widely used fuel in those days, because only a small amount could be found near the earth's surface. Most oil is trapped beneath the earth's surface.

Millions of years ago, the remains of dead plants and animals sank to the bottom of oceans, lakes, and swamps. The plant and animal matter was made up mainly of four chemical elements—nitrogen, oxygen, hydrogen, and carbon. Slowly, the plant and animal matter changed form. The weight of the water and of the matter as more of it fell to the bottom caused some of the change. The shifting movements of the earth also caused the plant and animal matter to change. Heat trapped beneath the earth's surface and chemical reactions changed the matter further. All of this happened over thousands—even millions—of years.

In time, the nitrogen and oxygen were forced out. That left the hydrogen and the carbon. Much of the hydrogen and carbon combined and turned into a liquid. The liquid became trapped in spaces inside the earth. That liquid is what we know today as petroleum—oil. It is a *hydrocarbon*—a compound of hydrogen and carbon.

History of Oil Use Oil may have been around for millions of years. Yet people have been using it in large amounts for only a short time. Just 100 years ago, wood and coal were much more important fuels than oil. They were plentiful and easier to obtain.

To reach large amounts of oil, people had to drill wells. The first oil wells were drilled in Europe in the 1600s. The first oil well in the United States was drilled in 1859. Still, there was little reason to drill for oil. There was plenty of wood for fuel, and there were few uses for oil.

In the late 1800s, a new invention—the automobile—appeared. It ran on fuels made from oil. Soon, many people were drilling for oil. Successful wells were drilled in Texas, Oklahoma, California, and Louisiana. (*See* **oil drilling.**)

As the use of cars grew in the 1920s, so did the need for oil. Between 1920 and 1930, the use of oil in the United States more than doubled. Today, the United States uses each year more than 15 times the amount of oil it used in 1920.

Finding Oil To find out where oil is likely to be, scientists study the layers of rock in the earth. They do this by setting off an explosion on the earth's surface. Then they record how the sound waves created by the explosion bounce off the deeper layers. They

know from experience that certain patterns in the sound waves sometimes point to deposits of oil. But they rarely find it. Fewer than one of every ten wells strikes oil.

Oil deposits are distributed all over the earth. Large deposits are under some seas and lakes—such as Lake Maracaibo in Venezuela, and the Persian Gulf in the Middle East.

The largest deposits of oil are found in the Middle East. Middle Eastern countries with large amounts of oil include Saudi Arabia, the United Arab Emirates, Iran, Iraq, Kuwait,

Oil from a well in Kansas (below) may end up as gasoline to run cars in Detroit (left).

and Egypt. The Soviet Union produces the most oil.

The United States is also one of the world's largest oil producers. But it uses more than it produces, so it must buy oil from other countries. It also uses more oil than any other country.

Scientists are not sure how much oil is in the earth now. They do know how much has already been discovered—about 28 trillion gallons (106 trillion liters).

Uses of Oil   The oil that comes from the ground is called *crude oil.* Crude oil may be deep golden-brown or light amber or cloudy blue-black, depending on what kind it is. Before the crude oil can be used, it must be *refined*—purified and separated into useful substances. This is done by heating the oil at a refinery.

Oil is used in the production of many substances besides fuels. Today, more than 3,000 products are made from oil. Some of them may surprise you. For example, oil goes into the making of paints, dyes, perfumes, car tires, shampoos, aspirin, and plastics such as stereo records and nylon.

Still, about half of the oil in the United States goes into making gasoline for cars. Thicker oil products are used as industrial fuels. Roads are paved with asphalt, a gummy oil product. Oil is also used to make home heating fuel.

Concerns About Oil   People have become concerned about the pollution caused by oil. When cars and trucks burn gasoline, they produce exhaust that contains pollutants. Oil refineries produce pollution, too. Occasionally, large oil tankers have accidents at sea. The oil they are carrying spills out and kills birds, fish, and other sea life. Sometimes, oil spills happen at wells that have been drilled at sea.

At the same time, people worry that the earth may run out of oil. In recent years, people have tried to use less of it. Today's car engines are built to burn less gasoline than they did in the 1960s. Many people lower the heat in their homes at night so their furnaces will not burn so much oil. Other energy resources—such as coal, solar energy, and nuclear energy—are being put to use. (*See* **energy.**)

Oil is refined into many *fractions*. Different fractions are used to make gasoline, fuel oil, plastics, lubricating oil, coke, asphalt, and other products.

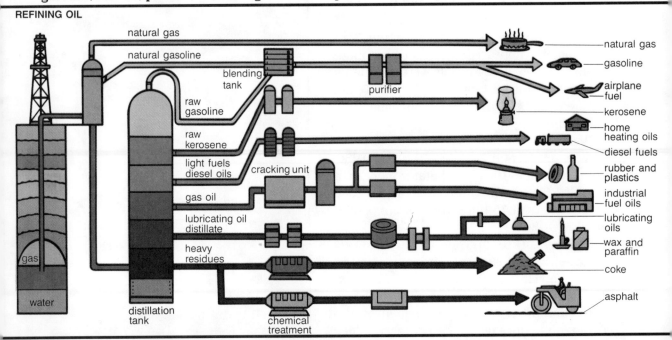

REFINING OIL

Oil spilled in the water is deadly to water birds and shore birds.

Still, the United States depends on oil for more than half of its energy needs. What would happen if it suddenly could not get enough oil?

That actually happened in 1973. Countries in the Middle East stopped sending oil to the United States. They wanted to force American companies to pay higher prices for oil. The prices of products made from oil immediately increased. People waited in line for hours to buy limited supplies of gasoline.

Most scientists estimate that there is enough oil to last at least 150 years. It may last longer if large new oil deposits are discovered. It will also last longer if people make an effort to conserve. That will give us time to learn how to make better use of other energy resources.

oil drilling

Petroleum oil is one of the earth's natural resources. It was formed over millions of years from decayed ocean plants and animals. Oil deposits exist all over the world. Some are far below the earth's surface. Others are less than 30 meters (100 feet) below. Some even ooze up to the surface.

People have taken oil from the earth's surface for thousands of years. They waterproofed boat hulls and roofs with the oil. They burned it for light and, much later, to power engines. Oil has also been used to heal wounds.

This huge oil refinery separates crude oil (see diagram at left). Part of the oil may be made into gasoline, part into heating oil, and part into other chemicals.

oil drilling

But not until 1859 did someone drill into the earth to reach oil. Edwin L. Drake set up his oil drill near Titusville, Pennsylvania. He used a *cable drill*—a heavy metal rod with a sharp tip. A metal cable lifted the rod and then dropped it. Each time it dropped, it dug deeper. He found oil 70 feet (21 meters) below the surface.

Over the next 40 years, oil wells were drilled in the United States and many other parts of the world. The invention of automobiles, oil-powered turbines, and other machines created a greater demand for oil. *Geologists*—scientists who study the structure of the earth—realized that large oil deposits were far below the earth's surface. They discovered that oil can usually be found around certain kinds of rock and rock formations.

Rotary drilling replaced cable drilling in the early 1900s. It is still used today. In rotary drilling, a *bit*—the end of a drill—is connected to lengths of pipe. The bit is round, with sharp teeth around the edge. As the bit turns, the teeth dig and cut away rock and soil. The bit has a hollow center. As the drill grinds deeper, mud is pumped down through the pipes and out of the bit. The mud does three jobs. It forces the torn rock and soil to the surface. It also keeps the bit greased. Finally, it keeps the walls of the *shaft*—the hole being drilled—from falling in. Once a well has been dug, the shaft is usually lined with metal before the oil is pumped up.

There are different bits for drilling through various kinds of soils and rocks. Some bits have industrial diamonds in the cutting teeth, to drill through the hardest rock.

The part of the well above the ground is the *oil rig*. It holds the machinery that operates the drill and that forces the mud down the shaft. The tall, towerlike part of the rig is the *derrick*. As the well is dug deeper, extra sections of pipe are attached through the top of the derrick. A modern oil-well may be more than 30,000 feet (9,000 meters) deep. Many lengths of pipe are used. When a bit

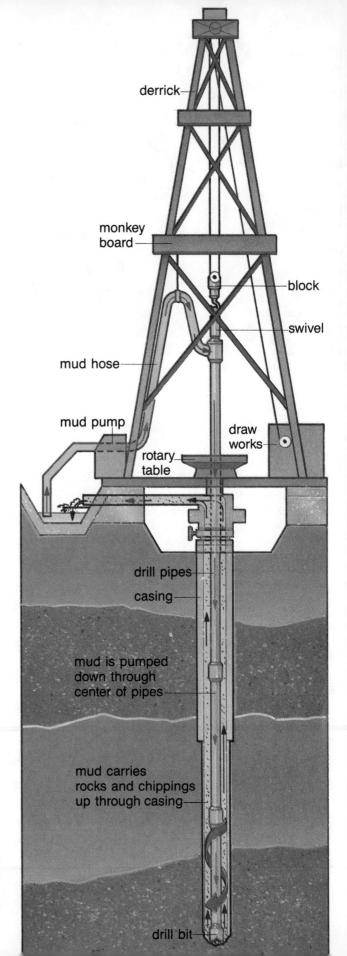

Offshore rigs are set up to drill wells underwater and to pump oil out of them.

has to be changed, the pipe is lifted up through the top of the derrick. Sections of the long pipe are removed, one by one, so that the bit can be brought up.

Compressed gases, such as methane, are trapped underground along with oil deposits. When drilling breaks through the earth above the deposits, these gases rush up the shaft and carry oil to the surface. After the gases escape, the oil is pumped out.

Geologists have used satellite and computer information to find new oil reserves under the ocean floor. *Marine drilling* or *offshore drilling* is done from huge ocean platforms. The largest platforms may weigh nearly 1 million tons (900,000 metric tons) and can be used in water more than 1,000 feet (300 meters) deep. Crews live and work on these platforms for weeks at a time, often more than 100 miles (160 kilometers) from land. Today, marine drilling goes on all over the world, even in the Arctic Ocean.

See also oil.

O'Keeffe, Georgia

Georgia O'Keeffe was an American artist. She painted natural objects, especially flowers, shells, rocks, and animal bones. She also painted scenes of New Mexico's mountains and desert.

O'Keeffe was born in November 1887, in Sun Prairie, Wisconsin. By age ten, she had decided to become an artist. She studied art in Chicago and in New York City. Her teachers wanted her to copy the styles of earlier artists, but O'Keeffe wanted to paint in her own way.

In 1912, O'Keeffe moved to Texas to work. In Texas, she painted as she wanted. Some of her artwork was *abstract*—a composition of colors and shapes. At other times, she drew realistic scenes of the Texas landscape.

A friend showed O'Keeffe's drawings to Alfred Stieglitz, a well-known photographer who also ran an art gallery in New York City. He liked her drawings and exhibited them in 1916. O'Keeffe moved to New York City in 1918 and married Stieglitz in 1924. She began painting close-up views of flowers. The clear colors and precise forms make you feel you are inside the flowers.

In 1929, O'Keeffe visited New Mexico. She liked the endless landscape and desert light so much that she eventually settled there. O'Keeffe died in 1986. You can see her paintings in many art museums.

The Mountain, New Mexico by O'Keeffe.

Georgia O'Keeffe. THE MOUNTAIN, NEW MEXICO. (1931). OIL ON CANVAS. 30 × 36 INCHES. COLLECTION OF WHITNEY MUSEUM OF AMERICAN ART. PURCHASE. 32.14

Oklahoma

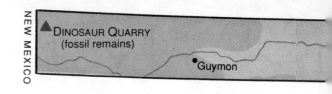

Capital: Oklahoma City
Area: 69,956 square miles   (181,186 square kilometers)   (18th-largest state)
Population (1980): 3,025,487   (1985): about 3,301,000   (25th-largest state)
Became a state: November 16, 1907   (46th state)

Oklahoma is an oil-rich state in the south-central United States. The name "Oklahoma" means "Land of the Red People" in the language of the Choctaw Indians.

Oklahoma is bordered by Kansas and Colorado on the north, Texas on the south, Missouri and Arkansas on the east, and New Mexico on the west. On a map, it has a roughly rectangular shape plus a long, narrow "panhandle" pointing west.

Land The Oklahoma Panhandle is high and dry. The highest point in the state is Black Mesa—4,973 feet (1,516 meters)—in the far northwestern corner of the Panhandle. Most of the rest of Oklahoma is rolling grasslands. The rugged Ouachita Mountains are in the southeastern part of the state.

The Red River forms Oklahoma's southern border. The Arkansas River drains the northeastern part of the state. Both flow into the Mississippi. (*See* **Mississippi River.**)

Several of Oklahoma's rivers have been dammed to create artificial lakes. These reservoirs are used for irrigation, hydroelectric power, and recreation.

Oklahoma's summers are usually long and hot. The temperature can reach 120° F (49° C). Winters are generally short, with little snow. The fertile soil is good for growing wheat, sorghum, corn, cotton, and peanuts. Cattle-raising is another important agricultural activity. Lumber comes from forests in the east and southeast.

Oklahoma's most valuable resources are petroleum and natural gas. Oil wells have been operating in Oklahoma since 1897.

History Many tribes of Plains Indians used to live in what is now Oklahoma. The first European to explore the area was the Spaniard Francisco Vásquez de Coronado. He passed through in 1541, looking for gold.

About 150 years later, the French claimed all of the land drained by the Mississippi River, including what is now Oklahoma. In 1803, the United States bought Oklahoma from France as part of the Louisiana Purchase. (*See* **Louisiana Purchase.**)

Five Indian tribes living east of the Mississippi River were forced by the government to give up their lands to white settlers. They were the Cherokee, Choctaw, Creek, Chickasaw, and Seminole Indians—the "Five Civilized Tribes." These tribes had lived close to white people for a long time. They had gone to mission schools and adopted many of the customs of their white neighbors. Between 1820 and 1840, they were marched to Oklahoma, following what came to be known as the "Trail of Tears." Once in Oklahoma, they, unlike the buffalo-hunting Plains Indians, built homes and farmed the land. Few white people were allowed into the area.

Then, in 1889, part of western Oklahoma was opened up for white settlement. The land was divided up into 160-acre (64-hectare) tracts. Each tract was given, free, to the first man to reach it after noon on April 22, 1889. Some 50,000 people rushed to Oklahoma. Some of the settlers tried to reach their tracts before noon. They were called "sooners." That is why Oklahoma's nickname is the "Sooner State."

More settlers followed. The western part of the area was organized as the Oklahoma Territory. The eastern part was still the Indian Territory. In 1907, the two territories were united into the state of Oklahoma.

KANSAS

Alva

Great Salt Plains Lake

Ponca City

Bartlesville

Miami

Neosho River

Lake of the Cherokees

MISSOURI

Woodward

Cimarron River

North Canadian River

Enid

Keystone Lake

GRAVE OF WILL ROGERS ▲

Claremore

Fort Gibson Lake

OZARK PLATEAU

Stillwater

Tulsa

OFTEN CALLED THE "OIL CAPITAL OF THE WORLD"

Tenkiller Ferry Lake

O   K   L   A   H   O   M   A

Canadian River

Guthrie

Cushing

Sapulpa

Muskogee

Okmulgee

Scissortail flycatcher

TEXAS

Clinton

El Reno

River

Oklahoma City ★

Midwest City

Shawnee

Seminole

Eufaula lake

Washita River

UNIVERSITY OF OKLAHOMA ▲

Norman

Chickasha

Ada

McAlester

OUACHITA MOUNTAINS

ARKANSAS

Altus

Lawton

Duncan

Pauls Valley

▲ CHICKASAW NATIONAL RECREATION AREA

OUACHITA NATIONAL FOREST ▲

Red River

Ardmore

Durant

Lake Texoma

TEXAS

▲ Historical Sites and Points of Interest

ELEVATION   Feet

3000 —	5000
2000 —	3000
1500 —	2000
1000 —	1500
600 —	1000
300 —	600

0   MILES   40

Mistletoe

Indian children, who represent Oklahoma's past, will help shape its future, too.

People   More than one-tenth of all the Indians in the United States live in Oklahoma. They make up almost 6 percent of Oklahoma's population. Only the state of Arizona has a larger Indian population.

Two-thirds of all Oklahomans live in cities. Almost one-third of the population lives in or near Oklahoma City, the state capital. It is also the major commercial, agricultural, and transportation center. Tulsa is the second-largest city.

About one-third of Oklahomans work in manufacturing. Most people work in petroleum refining. Food products and machinery—especially oil-field machinery—come next. Although petroleum mining brings in the most money, it does not involve as many workers as other industries.

75

olive

The olive is a small, oval, oily fruit that grows on a tree. Ripe olives are purplish black. Unripe olives are a dull yellowish green. The olive is a *drupe*—a fruit with one seed. Olives are eaten as fruit or crushed for their oil.

An olive tree can grow as tall as 25 feet (7.5 meters). Its trunk is short, and its branches are twisted. The leaves are green with silver-gray undersides.

Olive trees grow well in hot, dry climates. They produce more fruit if there is a moderate amount of rain. They begin bearing fruit when they are four or five years old, and can live for hundreds of years. Most varieties are *alternate bearing*—they yield large crops every other year.

Fresh-picked olives have an unpleasant taste. They are washed in a weak lye solution to remove the bitterness before being packed for eating or pressed for oil.

An olive is about one-fourth oil. Olives for oil are picked just as they ripen. After the bitterness is washed away, the fruit and seed are crushed and pressed. The first pressing gives the best oil. Oil from the last pressing is used in soaps, cosmetics, and other non-food products.

Both black olives and green olives are eaten as fruit. Black olives have a sweeter taste, because they are ripe when picked.

Olives grow on trees. They must be processed before they are good to eat.

To prepare olives for eating, they are first placed in salty water for several months. Then they are washed in a solution of lye and packed in salty water in jars or cans. Sometimes the seeds are removed. The olive may be stuffed with an almond or a small strip of sweet, red pimiento pepper.

People have been growing olive trees and eating their fruit for thousands of years. Scientists believe that the first olive trees grew in western Asia near the Mediterranean Sea. From there, the trees spread to the region surrounding the Mediterranean.

Today, Spain and Italy produce over half of the world's olives. The olive is also an important crop in Greece, Turkey, Tunisia, and Portugal. Spaniards brought the olive tree to the Americas. In the United States, most olives are grown in California, and they are grown for eating. In the Mediterranean countries, most olives are used to make oil.

Olympic Games

Every four years, people everywhere turn their eyes toward a big event. That event is the Olympic Games. Young men and women from nearly every country in the world come together to compete in many sports.

The Olympics are among the world's most important sporting events. Actually, there are two separate Olympic Games—the Summer Games and the Winter Games. The Summer Games usually take place in July and August. The Winter Games usually take place in February.

Both Summer and Winter Games last for about two weeks. They begin with colorful opening ceremonies. Athletes parade under the flags of their nations. There is music and dancing. Four weeks before the games open, runners begin carrying a lighted torch from Olympia, Greece, to the country where the games will be held. The torch is handed in a relay from one runner to the next. The last runner carries it into the stadium, where it is used to light the Olympic Flame. This officially opens the games.

In the opening ceremonies, athletes carry the flags of their countries. The Olympic symbol is five interlocking circles (left).

The Summer Games are the larger of the two events. Thousands of athletes from more than 140 nations compete in more than 20 sports. Track and field, swimming, gymnastics, and soccer are among the popular events. Athletes also compete in archery, boxing, cycling, volleyball, horseback riding, and rowing.

More than 1,000 athletes participate in the Winter Games. They compete in skiing, figure skating, speed skating, ice hockey, tobogganing, and bobsledding.

The winner of an Olympic event receives a gold medal. A silver medal goes to the second-place winner, and the third-place winner receives a bronze medal. Winning an Olympic medal is one of the greatest achievements in sports.

The Olympic Games are held in different places all over the world. Sometimes, they are held in North America. The 1984 Summer Games took place in Los Angeles, California, in the United States. The 1988 Winter Games were held in Calgary, Alberta,

in Canada. Several million people come to see the games in person. More than a billion people—about one out of five in the entire world—watch some part of the Olympic Games on television.

History of the Olympics The first Olympic contest was held in Olympia, a town in Greece, in the year 776 B.C. The event was part of a festival to honor the ancient Greek god Zeus. It was a running race of about 200 yards (182 meters)—a small event compared to today's games. Contestants came from Greek cities, and only men could take part or watch the race.

The ancient Olympics were held every four years for about 1,100 years. By this time, Greece had been conquered by other peoples, and the Olympics were no longer a religious festival. Then, in A.D. 393 the games were outlawed.

In 1894 Baron Pierre de Coubertin, a Frenchman, had an idea. Why not have a special athletic event to promote world peace and friendship? He presented his idea at a

Swimming (left) and track and field (above) are two types of events at the Summer Games.

meeting of international sports leaders. Everyone agreed that it was a good idea.

The first modern Olympic Games were held in 1896. To honor the ancient Greek games, they were held in Athens, Greece. As in the ancient Olympics, only male athletes competed. Women first competed four years later, in the 1900 Olympics.

Since then, the Olympics have been held every four years except for the years 1916, 1940, and 1944, when many of the countries of the world were at war. The first Winter Games were held in 1924.

Politics at the Olympics As Baron de Coubertin hoped, the Olympics have helped bring many nations together in friendship. But some people see the games as a contest between countries. They count how many medals are won by the large nations, such as the United States and the Soviet Union.

The United States did not send teams to the 1980 Summer Games in the Soviet Union. President Jimmy Carter kept U.S. teams at home to protest the Soviet invasion of Afghanistan. Four years later, the Soviets did not send a team to the Summer Games in the United States. Some people worry that using the games for such political protests may lead to the end of the Olympic Games.

Great Olympic Moments Most people watch the games to see great performances by the finest athletes of many countries. Over the years, there have been many amazing performances. One of the most wonderful moments in sports occurred at the Olympics in 1936. Jesse Owens, a black American track-and-field star, won four gold medals. (*See* **Owens, Jesse.**)

In 1972, the American swimmer Mark Spitz won seven gold medals—more than anyone had ever won in a single Olympics. Spitz was only 17 years old. In 1980, Eric Heiden, a U.S. speed skater, won five gold medals and set Olympic records in all five

Bobsledding (above) is an exciting event in the Winter Games. Gymnastics is a popular indoor summer event.

events. At the 1984 games, another American athlete, Carl Lewis, won four gold medals in the same events in which Jesse Owens had competed.

Of course, U.S. athletes are not the only ones who have pleased and excited Olympic fans. In 1952, Emil Zatopek of Czechoslovakia amazed the world. He won two long-distance running races—the 5,000 meters (about 3.1 miles) and the 10,000 meters (6.2 miles). Then he ran the marathon, a race of more than 26 miles. He had never run a marathon before, but he won a gold medal in that event as well.

In 1972, Olga Korbut, a young gymnast from the Soviet Union, became an Olympic star. Four years later, another gymnast, Nadia Comaneci of Romania, became the first gymnast ever to receive a perfect mark of 10.0 in the Olympics.

A New Look at the Olympics For many years, only *amateur* athletes—those who are not paid to play—were allowed to compete in the Olympics. Professional athletes—those who are paid, such as major-league baseball players—were not allowed to enter. Baron de Coubertin wanted the Olympics to be for athletes who train and compete for the love of sport, not for money.

Today, however, many athletes spend nearly all their time training, while their expenses are paid by someone else. Many people hope the Olympics will soon be open to all athletes, both professionals and amateurs. The athletes would not be paid to play in the Olympics. They would compete in the hope of winning an Olympic medal—still one of the greatest honors in sports.

Oman, *see* **Middle East**

omnivore, *see* **animal**

Ontario

Capital: Toronto
Area: 412,580 square miles (1,068,582 square kilometers) (2nd-largest province)
Population (1981): 8,625,107 (1985): about 9,023,900 (largest province)
Became a province: July 1, 1867 (one of four original provinces)

Ontario is Canada's second-largest province and its business and manufacturing center. More people live in Ontario than any other Canadian province. Stretching farther south than the rest of Canada, Ontario is the nation's gateway to the United States.

Ontario is in the center of Canada. The northern part of the province touches Hudson Bay and James Bay. Southern Ontario lies along four of the five Great Lakes—Superior, Huron, Erie, and Ontario. From Lake Ontario, the St. Lawrence River provides a link to the Atlantic Ocean. Quebec Province is Ontario's neighbor to the east. To the west lies the Province of Manitoba.

Land   About half of Ontario is covered by the *Canadian Shield*—an area of low, rocky hills that was once a mountain chain. Northern Ontario is blanketed with forests of pine, spruce, and balsam. More than 250,000 lakes and rivers are found here, as well as large deposits of minerals. Trees from the forests provide wood used to make paper, including *newsprint*—the paper on which newspapers are printed. Mines near the city of Sudbury produce a quarter of the world's supply of nickel. Large amounts of copper and platinum are also mined here. Iron ore, gold, uranium, and lead are among the other minerals found in Ontario.

Southern Ontario has a mild climate and fertile soil. There are dairy farms along Lake Ontario and the St. Lawrence River. Many farmers also raise cattle for beef. Grapes, apples, pears, and raspberries are among the fruits grown in the area drained by the Niagara River. Tobacco is the major crop on the

farms along Lake Erie. Ontario leads the rest of Canada in the production of eggs and poultry.

Power plants on the Niagara and other rivers harness the energy of water to make electricity. The power these plants supply is called *hydroelectricity*. (*See* **Niagara Falls**.)

People One out of 20 Ontarians work as farmers, and about one out of four work in manufacturing. Half of all of Canada's manufactured goods come from Ontario. The province produces most of the steel made in Canada, as well as most of the nation's automobiles, aircraft, and rubber and electrical goods.

Most of Ontario's people live in the southern part of the province. Toronto, a port city on Lake Ontario, is the capital of Ontario. The city of Ottawa, near the Quebec border, is the Canadian capital. (*See* **Toronto** and **Ottawa**.)

About two-thirds of the people in Ontario are of British descent, and about a tenth are of French origin. There are large numbers of immigrants from other European countries, including Germany, the Netherlands, the

Northern Ontario has many beautiful lakes for summer fishing and boating.

Scandinavian nations, and Poland. Ontario has the largest Indian population of all the Canadian provinces. Over 60,000 descendants of the Cree, Ojibwa, Algonquian, Iroquois, and other tribes live in Ontario today.

History The Huron, Chippewa, and Iroquois Indians were living throughout Ontario before the first Europeans arrived. Samuel de Champlain, a Frenchman, explored southern Ontario in 1615. When he reported that the area was rich in fur-bearing animals, more Frenchmen arrived, eager to make money in the fur trade. In 1639, French missionaries built a mission settlement named Fort Sainte Marie among the Huron Indians.

British exploration of Ontario began around Hudson Bay. The first British settlement was named Moose Factory. It was located on James Bay. The British mostly worked for the Hudson's Bay Company, a trading firm that claimed all of the land drained by Hudson Bay. The company's workers built forts and small settlements in the area. They gave the Indians blankets, guns, and clothing in exchange for furs.

France was forced to give its Canadian land to Britain at the end of the French and Indian War in 1763. The area remained largely unsettled until the end of the American Revolution in 1784. Then thousands of American colonists who had remained loyal to Great Britain during the war moved to Canada. Later, more settlers came to Ontario from the United States and Great Britain. In 1867, Ontario, Quebec, Nova Scotia, and New Brunswick united to form the Dominion of Canada.

Today, millions of people visit Ontario each year to go fishing, hunting, camping, and boating. Visitors also enjoy Ontario's annual Stratford Festival of plays by William Shakespeare and others, winter carnivals, and beautiful Horseshoe Falls—the larger part of Niagara Falls. (*See* **Niagara Falls**.)

Ontario, Lake, *see* Great Lakes

Where the Wild Things Are is an opera based on a story for children. The author, Maurice Sendak, designed the costumes and sets for the opera.

opera

An opera is a play in which the characters are played by singers. Nearly all the words are sung, not spoken. Some of the world's most beautiful music is in operas. Opera lovers flock to large cities to see and hear opera. They also listen to radio and television broadcasts and collect recordings of their favorite operas.

An opera is often performed in a large auditorium called an *opera house*. An opera house may seat more than 2,000 people. Between the audience and the stage is a space called the *pit*, where the orchestra plays during the opera. The large stage contains elaborate *sets*—painted scenery. It can be lit with powerful lights. The singers wear makeup and costumes. Some operas have a chorus and dancers as well as the solo singers.

Most operas tell stirring, eventful stories. The characters express strong feelings of love, joy, hatred, fear, and sadness. The music expresses these feelings, too.

Opera Music An opera opens with an *overture*—a musical introduction played by the orchestra before the curtain goes up.

When the curtain rises, the story begins. The orchestra continues to play, accompanying the singers. Long operas may have three, four, or even five acts, with intermissions in between.

An opera features solo singers who play important characters in the story. Soloists in most operas sing in two styles. *Recitative* is a kind of singing much like ordinary speech. The performers use recitative when they are "speaking" to each other about everyday things.

When characters want to express strong feelings, they break into a song called an *aria*. During an aria, a singer can show off a beautiful voice and acting ability.

Sometimes, two or more characters sing at once. There are many famous duets, trios, and quartets in opera music. Often, the singers express different feelings or opinions.

The orchestra's performance is very important to the success of the opera. An opera orchestra has many of the same instruments as a symphony orchestra. But it is smaller, so the singers can be heard over the music. The conductor of the orchestra conducts the singers as well as the musicians. The singers watch the conductor's beat from their places onstage. (*See* **orchestra.**)

Opera Stories A book containing the words in an opera is called a *libretto*. Often it has the words both in the original language and an English translation. Many operas are written and sung in Italian or German. A smaller number are in English, French, Russian, or some other language. Opera fans often bring librettos to the opera so that they can follow the words being sung.

There are two kinds of opera. *Comic operas* are usually about people in love. Comic operas end happily, often with a wedding. One of the most famous comic operas is *The Marriage of Figaro,* by Mozart. (*See* **Mozart, Wolfgang Amadeus.**)

Tragic operas may also be about people in love, but they end unhappily. Many of the most popular operas—such as *Carmen, Aida, Madame Butterfly,* and *Tristan and Isolde*—are tragic operas.

Opera History The first operas were written by Italian composers around the year 1600. These operas were very serious, and their stories moved very slowly. They were performed in the courts of kings and nobles. Only men and boys sang them. By the 1700s, Italian opera was very popular, and composers in other parts of Europe were writing music for them.

Late in the 1700s, composers began to use stories that were more realistic and moved more quickly. Women began to sing in operas, too. The first great composer of this new kind of opera was Mozart.

The 1800s were the Golden Age of opera. Many of the great composers of this period were from Italy. Giuseppe Verdi was perhaps the greatest. Many of his operas, such as *Rigoletto* and *Il Trovatore,* are still performed by opera companies around the world. Giacomo Puccini was the most popular opera composer of the late 1800s and early 1900s. He wrote *Madame Butterfly,* the sad story of a Japanese woman whose American husband leaves her.

Don Giovanni

Falstaff

Madame Butterfly

Faust

The leading roles in four popular operas.

There were other great opera composers outside Italy. In Germany, Richard Wagner wrote grand operas in the German language. He often used stories from German myths.

American composers have also written operas. Perhaps the most famous is *Porgy and Bess* by George Gershwin. It tells the story of poor black people in the South. "Summertime" and other songs from the opera have been popular for more than 50 years. (*See* **Gershwin, George.**)

See also **singing.**

opinion poll

An opinion poll is a survey taken to find out what a large number of people think about a particular person, product, or question. Politicians study opinion polls to see how voters feel about issues. Opinion polls taken before elections are used to predict the winner. Advertising agencies and businesses use opinion polls to see if people like their products.

People who make up the questions, ask the questions, and collect the answers are called *pollsters.* Since the pollsters cannot possibly question everyone, they use a technique called *sampling.* They ask a small number of people—a sample of a larger group—the questions. People in the larger group usually have something in common, such as being pet owners, baseball fans, teenagers, or voters. The answers given by the sample reflect the opinions of the larger group.

Often, pollsters choose names by chance from a list. This is called *random sampling.* Pollsters may interview people by mail, by phone, or in person. Computers are usually used to count the results.

The Gallup Poll and the Harris Survey are two widely used opinion polls in the United States.

opossum

The opossum is a mammal that lives in the Western Hemisphere—North America, Central America, and South America. Opossums are *marsupials*—the female of most kinds has a pouch on her abdomen for her babies to stay in while they are nursing.

A female opossum may give birth to as many as 20 babies at a time. The newborn opossums are only 1 centimeter (½ inch) long. These tiny animals climb over the mother's body and into her pouch. There, they cling to her nipples and nurse. After five or six weeks, the babies are big enough to begin exploring. They climb out of the

pouch and stay outside for longer and longer periods. During this time, they often travel on their mother's back. They use their feet to hold on to her fur, or they wrap their tails tightly around her tail.

An adult opossum is about the size of a house cat. It has grayish white fur, a pointed nose, and a long hairless tail. It usually rests during the day and searches for food at night. An opossum uses its tail to hold on to branches as it climbs up and down trees looking for insects, fruit, and other food. It rests hanging by its tail from a tree branch. The opossum is at home on the ground, too. It makes its home in hollow trees or in holes in the ground. It can often be found in woods and fields near people's homes.

When an opossum thinks it is in danger, it gives off an awful-smelling liquid. It may also roll over, stay still, and appear dead. This is the source of the expression "playing 'possum."

There are about 65 kinds of opossums. Most live in Central America and South America. Only the *common opossum* lives in North America. A few, such as the *murine opossum,* do not have pouches to protect the babies.

A young opossum rests by hanging by its tail from a tree branch.

Zubin Mehta (standing) conducts the New York Philharmonic Orchestra in a performance featuring violinist Itzak Perlman (second from left).

Some kinds of opossums spend much of their lives in water. The *yapok* is a water opossum. It has webbed back feet and a very long, flat tail. These help it move through the water. The yapok lives in forests in northern South America. During the day, it rests in its burrow on the bank of a river. At night, it comes out to feed on fish, crayfish, and water insects. A yapok's burrow is often easy to spot, because there is usually a pile of crayfish shells outside the entrance.

orchestra

An orchestra is a large group of musical instruments that play together. Different kinds of groups can be called orchestras. We most often use the word to describe a group that has mostly stringed instruments. A band has mostly wind instruments—brass and woodwinds—and percussion instruments—drums, cymbals, and triangles. (*See* **band**.)

Besides performing in concert halls, orchestras provide the background music for many movies, television shows, and commercials. They *accompany*—play with—popular singers on recordings and broadcasts. In Broadway musicals and other musical shows, an orchestra plays from a *pit*—a place between the stage and the audience. Opera companies and ballet companies perform with orchestras.

The Symphony Orchestra A symphony orchestra is a large orchestra that has instruments in the string, woodwind, brass, and percussion families. Some symphony orchestras, such as the Boston Pops, play popular music from movies, shows, and popular recordings. Most symphony orchestras play *classical music*—the music written by great composers over the last 300 years.

A symphony orchestra is led by a *music director*. The director helps choose the music to be played, practices with the orchestra,

SYMPHONY ORCHESTRA

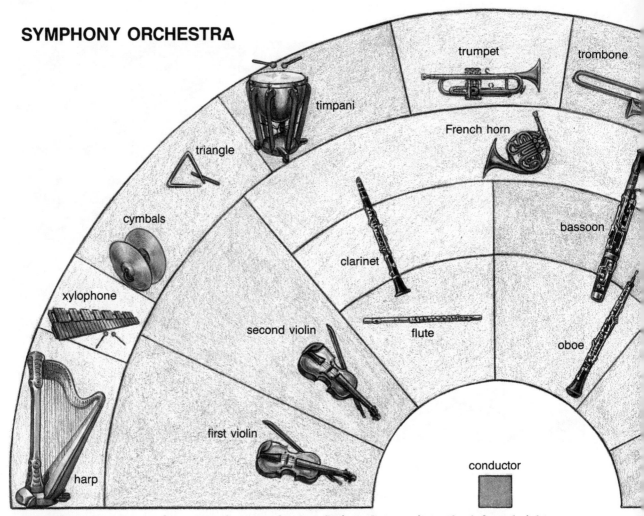

trumpet

trombone

timpani

French horn

triangle

cymbals

bassoon

clarinet

xylophone

second violin

flute

oboe

first violin

conductor

harp

A seating arrangement for a symphony orchestra. String players sit to the left and right. Woodwind players sit in the center. Brass and percussion players sit in the rear.

and conducts many of its concerts. Symphony conductors are among the most famous musicians in the world. The Italian conductor Arturo Toscanini conducted orchestras in Europe and the United States until his death in 1953. Leonard Bernstein was music director of the New York Philharmonic and is also famous as a composer. Conductors direct the music for operas or ballets, too.

Arranging the Orchestra The music director arranges a symphony orchestra on the stage. The diagram on this page shows one common way this is done. People playing the same instruments or instruments in the same family sit together.

In a symphony orchestra, there are more violins than any other instrument. As you

can see in the diagram, they sit on the left of the conductor. Those nearest the edge of the stage are the *first violins*. They play the highest-pitched part in the string section. Those closer to the middle are the *second violins*. They play the second highest-pitched part. Often, the first and second violins play different parts of the same piece.

On the right of the conductor are the other stringed instruments—the violas, cellos, and double basses. All of these instruments have a lower pitch than the violins. A listener seated in front of the orchestra hears the higher notes from the left and the lower notes from the right.

In the middle of the orchestra, in front of the conductor, are the woodwinds—flutes, oboes, clarinets, and bassoons. The French

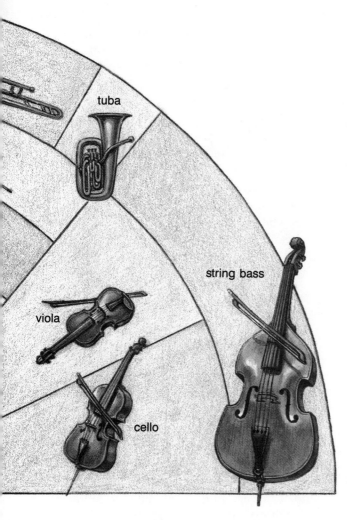

tuba

string bass

viola

cello

A **Symphony Concert** A symphony orchestra often plays a variety of music in a concert. The concert may open with a light, exciting number, followed by a *concerto*—a piece for a solo instrument and orchestra. The soloist may play the piano, violin, or some other instrument. (*See* **concerto.**)

An intermission in the middle of the concert gives the players and the audience a chance to rest. In the second half of the concert, the orchestra may play a long piece for orchestra alone. A *symphony* is one kind of piece for orchestra. (*See* **symphony.**)

The size of an orchestra may change according to the requirements of the music. Some pieces were written for a small orchestra—a *chamber orchestra*—or sometimes for only stringed instruments or woodwinds. Others were written for such a large orchestra that a conductor may add players in some sections.

See also **musical instrument.**

---

ore

Ore is soil or rock that contains good amounts of one or more metals. A few metals—such as gold, copper, and mercury—are sometimes found free in nature—not combined with other elements. But most metals are found combined with other elements in ores. Many ores contain a metal combined with oxygen. When these ores are heated with carbon, the oxygen and carbon combine and leave the metal free.

Ancient peoples learned how to separate copper, lead, tin, and iron from ores. Other metals, such as aluminum and titanium, have only been discovered in the past 200 years. At first, they could not be separated from their ores without great expense. This made aluminum, for example, more expensive than gold. About 100 years ago, electricity was used to separate aluminum ores. Today, aluminum, made from a common ore called *bauxite,* is one of the least expensive metals.

See also **metal; mineral;** and **rock.**

horns are also in this section. These are really brass instruments, but they often play with the woodwinds, so they sit near them.

In the back of the orchestra, at the right center, are the brass instruments—trumpets, trombones, and sometimes one or two tubas. The brass instruments can be loud and exciting.

In the back at the left are the percussion instruments. Most drums, triangles, cymbals, and tambourines play only one pitch, but they give movement and excitement to the music. The timpani player stands at the very back of the orchestra in front of three huge kettledrums, each tuned to a different pitch. The deep *boom* of the timpani can be heard even when all the other instruments are playing loudly.

Oregon

Capital: Salem
Area: 97,073 square miles (251,419 square kilometers) (10th-largest state)
Population (1980): 2,633,156 (1985): about 2,687,000 (30th-largest state)
Became a state: February 14, 1859 (33rd state)

Oregon is a state in the northwestern United States. It is known for its beautiful, rugged coast and evergreen forests. Oregon is bordered by Washington State on the north, by Nevada and California on the south, by Idaho on the east, and by the Pacific Ocean on the west. The Columbia River forms most of the northern boundary. On the eastern boundary the Snake River has cut Hells Canyon, the deepest canyon in the United States. It is 40 miles (64 kilometers) long and up to 8,032 feet (2,448 meters) deep.

Land Much of Oregon is mountainous. The low, rolling Coast Range is in the western part of the state, near the Pacific coast. The Willamette River Valley separates the Coast Range from the Cascade Mountain Range. The Cascades have many tall mountains, including Mount Hood, the highest point in Oregon. It rises 11,239 feet (3,426 meters) above sea level. The Cascades also have deep valleys and beautiful lakes. Crater Lake, the deepest lake in the United States, is 1,932 feet (589 meters) deep.

Most of the eastern two-thirds of Oregon is the Columbia Plateau. The plateau is not completely flat. Mountains rise from it, and rivers and valleys cut into it.

The southern part of the plateau is dry and desertlike. Parts receive only 8 inches (20 centimeters) of rain a year. But western Oregon is wet. In some years, it receives 130 inches (330 centimeters) of rain.

Oregon is rich in natural resources. Forests—Oregon's most important natural resource—cover about half of the state. Oregon has great numbers of fish. Salmon, which migrate from the ocean to freshwater breeding grounds in rivers and streams, are very valuable. Some of Oregon's rivers have been dammed to create lakes. They supply water for hydroelectricity, irrigation, and recreation. Channels are built around the dams so the salmon can still migrate.

The soils of the Willamette and other valleys make excellent farmlands. The desert areas become productive with irrigation. About a third of Oregon's land is used for agriculture. Wheat, other grains, and hay are the chief crops. Potatoes, fruits, nuts, and vegetables are also important.

History Chinook, Paiute, and other Indian tribes lived in the area. By the 1700s, Russians, Frenchmen, Englishmen, and Spaniards were exploring Oregon. Canadian and British trappers and traders controlled the region by the early 1800s. They wanted furs, especially beaver and sea otter. They did not want farmers to come into their territory, but could not keep them away. Americans began arriving in the Willamette Valley in 1834. In 1846, the United States and England signed a treaty that created the Oregon Territory and made it part of the United States. The Oregon Territory included what are now Oregon, Idaho, Washington, and part of Wyoming and Montana.

People Today, two-thirds of Oregon's people live in cities, mostly in the Willamette Valley. Portland is near where the Willamette River joins the Columbia River. It is the state's largest city and the chief trade center for all of the northwestern states.

Eugene, 120 miles (193 kilometers) south of Portland, is the state's second-largest city. Eugene has canneries and meat-packing plants, and it is the home of the University of Oregon.

Salem, the state capital, is also in the Willamette Valley, between Portland and Eugene. It is Oregon's third-largest city.

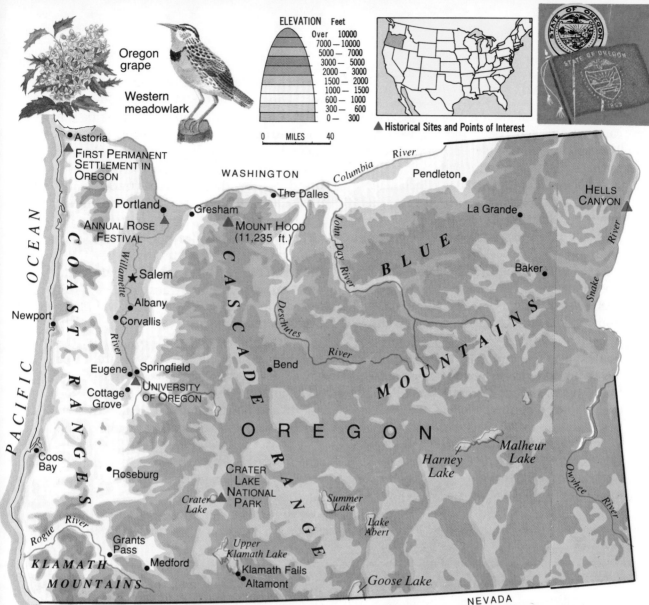

Oregon grape

Western meadowlark

ELEVATION Feet

Over	10000
7000 —	10000
5000 —	7000
3000 —	5000
2000 —	3000
1500 —	2000
1000 —	1500
600 —	1000
300 —	600
0 —	300

0   MILES   40

▲ Historical Sites and Points of Interest

PACIFIC OCEAN

Astoria
▲ FIRST PERMANENT SETTLEMENT IN OREGON

WASHINGTON

Columbia River

Portland
▲ ANNUAL ROSE FESTIVAL

Gresham

The Dalles

Pendleton

▲ MOUNT HOOD (11,235 ft.)

La Grande

HELLS CANYON ▲

Salem ★

Willamette River

BLUE MOUNTAINS

John Day River

Baker

Albany
Corvallis

Newport

COAST RANGES

Deschutes River

Snake River

Eugene   Springfield
▲ UNIVERSITY OF OREGON

Cottage Grove

Bend

CASCADE RANGE

OREGON

Coos Bay

Roseburg

CRATER LAKE NATIONAL PARK ▲

Crater Lake

Summer Lake

Harney Lake

Malheur Lake

Owyhee River

Rogue River

KLAMATH MOUNTAINS

Grants Pass

Medford

Upper Klamath Lake

Lake Abert

Klamath Falls
Altamont

Goose Lake

NEVADA

CALIFORNIA

The Pacific shore in Oregon is rugged and quiet.

Oregon's major industries are forestry and the manufacture of forest products. A fifth of all of the lumber cut in the United States comes from Oregon. Oregon produces about half of all the plywood in the nation. Oregon wood is used for buildings, railroad ties, furniture, pulp and paper, and telephone poles.

The state's second-biggest industry is the growing and processing of food. More than 100 factories freeze, can, or preserve food in other ways. Catching and processing fish and other seafood are other important industries.

Many Oregonians work in the tourist industry. The beauty of the land and the many opportunities for outdoor sports attract 100 million visitors a year to Oregon.

Oregon Trail

The Oregon Trail was a long, rugged road carved by wagon trains moving westward. The trail ran from Independence, Missouri, to the Oregon Country of the Pacific Northwest—about 2,000 miles (3,200 kilometers). It wound through prairies, deserts, and mountains. During the 1840s, thousands of pioneers journeyed west on this bumpy dirt road.

Early Settlements The Oregon Country was an enormous area. It stretched from the Pacific Ocean to the Rocky Mountains, and from the northern edge of California to Alaska. Meriwether Lewis and William Clark had explored parts of the Pacific Northwest for the United States in the early 1800s. Both the United States and Great Britain claimed parts of the Oregon Country. (*See* **Lewis and Clark Expedition.**)

American fur trappers followed Lewis and Clark into the Oregon Country and set up trading posts. During the 1830s, American missionaries founded settlements in Oregon's Willamette River Valley. These early settlers sent reports of Oregon's mild weather and fertile soil to friends and relatives living east of the Mississippi River. By the 1840s, pioneer families were making the long journey west to the Oregon Country. There they hoped to farm the land and make new homes. The pioneers followed the path carved out by the explorers, traders, and missionaries. This route came to be known as the Oregon Trail.

The Way West The Oregon Trail began at Independence, Missouri, near the Missouri River. From Independence, the trail ran northwest to Fort Kearny in Nebraska. Next, it followed the wide, shallow Platte River and then the North Platte River west to Fort Laramie in Wyoming. From there, the trail continued along the North Platte River and its Sweetwater branch into the Rocky Mountains. At Fort Bridger, Wyoming, the trail turned north along the Snake River to Fort Hall and on to Fort Boise in Idaho. The last part of the trail crossed the Blue Mountains, passed Fort Walla Walla in Washington, and then followed the Columbia River to the Willamette Valley.

Life on the Oregon Trail was a mixture of adventure, hardship, and danger. The trip

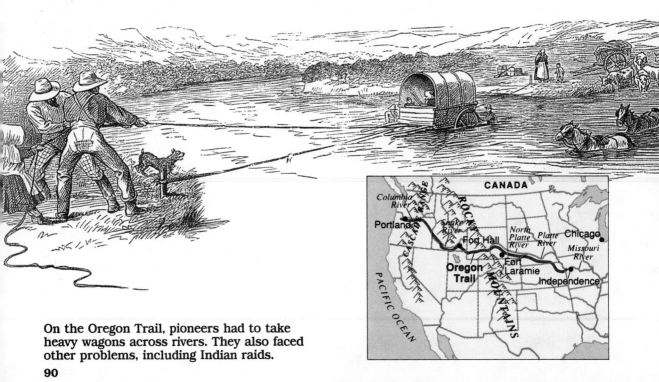

On the Oregon Trail, pioneers had to take heavy wagons across rivers. They also faced other problems, including Indian raids.

took about six months by covered wagon. The trail was a difficult one to travel. Rivers had to be crossed, even when they were flooded. Travelers often became ill from cholera and other diseases. The wagon train could not wait for them to feel better. Food and wood were sometimes hard to find. The settlers often found contaminated water holes when they needed fresh water for themselves and their animals. They were also attacked by Indians along the way.

At Independence, pioneer families gathered together in wagon trains—large groups of covered wagons. A wagon train might have as many as 120 wagons and 1,000 men, women, and children. Many families would bring livestock—oxen to pull the heavy wagons and cows for milking. Many travelers brought horses. In all, a wagon train might have about 1,400 animals.

Once the wagon train was formed, its members elected a captain to lead them. Men familiar with the trail were hired as guides. Larger wagon trains traveled in two sections. The train without livestock—called the *light column*—led the way. At the end of the day, the light column stopped to make camp. A few hours later, the slower part of the wagon train—called the *cow column*—reached the camp. When making camp, the pioneers would draw their wagons into a circle. This gave them added protection in case of Indian attacks.

By 1845, over 5,000 American pioneers had settled in the Oregon Country. The following year, the United States and Great Britain agreed on how the area should be divided. The border they drew is shared today by the United States and Canada.

In the years that followed, thousands more people followed the Oregon Trail west. Some went all the way to the Oregon Country. But many other settlers turned off the Oregon Trail and headed southwest on the California Trail. They were part of the gold rush to California after 1848.

See also **westward movement; Oregon; California Trail;** and **Gold Rush.**

Crosses with rounded ends—a Turkish design—are used in Orthodox churches.

Orthodox churches

The Orthodox churches are part of the world family of Christian churches. Today, about 59 million people are members of Orthodox churches in Greece, Russia, North America, Eastern Europe, and western Asia.

The early Christians belonged to one church and lived under the rule of the Roman Empire. In the year 330, the Roman emperor Constantine built the city of Constantinople on the present-day site of Istanbul, Turkey. Constantinople became the capital of the Roman Empire and the center of the Christian church in the east. Rome remained the center of the church in the west.

Eastern and Western Christians were divided by nationality, customs, and their ideas about the Christian faith. Over hundreds of years, the two sides drifted further apart. In 1054, the Eastern and Western churches finally separated from each other. The western Christians became known as Roman Catholics. The Eastern Christians formed the Orthodox churches, sometimes called the Eastern Orthodox churches.

The leaders of some of the oldest and most important Orthodox churches are called *patriarchs*. The patriarch of the Church of Constantinople is recognized as the leader of Orthodox Christians.

See also **Christianity.**

ostrich

The ostrich is the largest living bird. An adult may be over 2 meters (7 feet) tall and weigh over 135 kilograms (300 pounds).

An ostrich has a small head, a long neck, long legs, and big feet. Its huge eyes are fringed with long eyelashes. The male ostrich has black feathers on his body and white ones on his wings and tail. The female's feathers are all brown.

An ostrich cannot fly—its wings are too small. But it can run up to 64 kilometers (40 miles) per hour and outrun most of its enemies. Contrary to legend, the ostrich does not bury its head in the sand when frightened. If cornered, an ostrich kicks with its strong legs. The sharp nails on its toes can cause serious wounds.

Ostriches live on dry grasslands in Africa. They eat mainly plants, fruit, insects, mice, and lizards.

Ostriches usually live in small groups. One male mates with several females. Then he scrapes out a shallow hole in the ground where the females can lay their eggs. All the females lay their eggs in the same nest. There may be 30 or more eggs in one nest.

Ostriches lay the biggest eggs of all birds. The eggs each weigh about 1 kilogram (more than 2 pounds) and measure about 15 centimeters (6 inches) in diameter.

Ottawa

Ottawa is Canada's capital city and its fourth-largest urban area. Over 750,000 people live in and around Ottawa. The city is in the southeastern part of the province of Ontario. (*See* **Ontario.**)

The Dominion of Canada was created in 1867, and the new nation needed a capital. The capital had to be a place that people could travel to easily. It also had to be a place that could unite English-speaking and French-speaking Canadians. Canada's leaders chose Ottawa, a busy lumber town at the border of Ontario and Quebec provinces. Ottawa lies 248 miles (399 kilometers) northeast of Toronto and 127 miles (204 kilometers) west of Montreal. (*See* **Toronto** and **Montreal.**)

Life in Ottawa is mostly centered around the national government. Canada's lawmakers meet in three Parliament Buildings on a hill overlooking the Ottawa River. Next to Parliament is the Peace Tower, a monument to Canadians killed in World Wars I and II. Ottawa is also a center of the arts and education. It has several national museums and two universities. Parks along the Ottawa River and the Rideau Canal add to the city's beauty. In the summer, boats cruise up and down the canal. In the winter, people use the canal to skate to work.

These three ostriches escape from an enemy by galloping across the African grasslands. They can run as fast as 64 kilometers (40 miles) per hour.

This otter cracks open the shellfish by striking it with a rock.

otter

The otter is a mammal with a long, slender body, webbed feet, and a thick undercoat of fur protected by long, stiff guard hairs. Otters are excellent swimmers and spend most of their time in water. They are very playful animals, though they are also fierce hunters. There are two main kinds—river otters and sea otters.

River otters live in the Americas, Europe, Asia, and Africa. Their homes are in the ground near the water's edge. The entrance is usually below water level. Most river otters are 50 to 100 centimeters (20 to 40 inches) long, not counting their tails. They weigh 3.5 to 15 kilograms (10 to 33 pounds). River otters eat mainly fish, which they catch underwater and carry onto land to eat. When they are not busy hunting or eating, river otters often amuse themselves by sliding down riverbanks on their bellies or chasing each other around.

Sea otters live in the Pacific Ocean. They spend almost their entire lives in and around beds of seaweed near the coast. They eat shellfish and other sea animals. After catching food, a sea otter swims to the surface. It floats on its back and places the food on its belly. Using its front paws, it picks up one piece after another to eat. If lunch is a shellfish, the sea otter finds a rock to put on its belly and pounds the shellfish against the rock until the shell cracks open. Sea otters may be more than 1.2 meters (4 feet) long and weigh 35 kilograms (77 pounds).

Owens, Jesse

The motto of the Olympic Games is "Faster, higher, stronger." Jesse Owens lived up to that motto in a very special way.

Owens was a famous track-and-field athlete. He was born in Oakville, Alabama, in 1913. Even when he was very young, it was clear that he had great athletic ability. His talent helped win him a scholarship to Ohio State University.

One of the greatest moments in his career came in college. At a track meet in 1935, Owens was entered in four events—the 100-yard dash, the 200-yard dash, the long jump, and the 440-yard relay. He broke world records in three of those events and tied a world record in the fourth—all four in less than one hour!

But Owens's greatest achievement came the next year, at the Olympic Games. The 1936 Olympics were held in Berlin, Germany. At the time, Germany was ruled by the Nazi party. It taught that white people were better than blacks, and that Germans

Jesse Owens won four gold medals in the 1936 Olympic Games.

were better than all other people. But Owens proved the Nazis wrong. He entered four events and finished first in each, winning four gold medals. He was by far the best athlete in the games.

See also **Olympic Games.**

---

owl

The owl is a *bird of prey.* Birds of prey live by hunting small animals. Owls catch insects, fish, reptiles, birds, and small mammals, especially mice and other rodents.

There are about 160 kinds of owls. Most kinds sleep during the day and hunt at night. Their huge eyes and excellent hearing help them find prey. Their powerful feet and large *talons*—sharp, curved claws—are used to grab and carry off their prey. A few kinds hunt during the day.

Owls have large heads and flat faces. Owls in the barn owl family have heart-shaped or triangular faces. Other kinds have rounder faces. Owls' eyes face forward and cannot move from side to side. When an owl wants to look to the side, it must turn its head. Some owls can turn their heads almost completely around, or even upside down!

The smallest owl is the *elf owl.* It is about 15 centimeters (6 inches) long. The largest, the *great gray owl,* is 76 centimeters (30 inches) long.

Much of an owl's size is made up of feathers. Owls have more feathers than most other birds. Their feathers protect them from very low temperatures in Arctic areas and from the sun's heat in tropical areas. The fluffy feathers make it possible for owls to fly quietly. The "ears" or "horns" that some owls have on their heads are really tufts of feathers.

The feathers of owls are often a mix of brown, gray, black, and white. This helps the owls blend into the background so that prey and enemies cannot see them. Owls that live in forests are mostly brown and gray, to blend in with the trees. The *snowy owl,* which lives in the Arctic, is white with black markings. It blends in with the snow-covered rocks.

Most owls live in trees. The *burrowing owl* lives in the ground. It digs a burrow or lives in one made by another animal. Barn owls may live in barns—or in any other kind of sheltered spot, including trees and burrows.

If you are out at night, you may hear owls calling. Each kind of owl has its own call. *Great horned owls* and *barred owls* hoot. *Screech owls* whistle. *Barking owls,* which live in Australia, can sound like dogs. Many owls answer imitations of their calls. Some will even move near people who are making owl sounds.

See also **birds of prey.**

A screech owl makes a whistling sound, and a horned owl hoots. The snowy owl's color hides it from its arctic enemies.

common screech owl

snowy owl

great horned owl

oxygen

Oxygen is a tasteless, odorless, and colorless gas. About one-fifth of the earth's atmosphere is oxygen. The earth's crust is almost half oxygen. Oxygen makes up about two-thirds of the human body. It is the third-most-abundant element in the universe—after hydrogen and helium.

Nearly every living thing needs oxygen. Land animals get oxygen by breathing air. Their lungs absorb the oxygen, and from the lungs, it enters the bloodstream. Water animals breathe through gills. The gills absorb oxygen dissolved in water. Both land and water animals exhale carbon dioxide. During *photosynthesis,* plants use sunlight, water, and carbon dioxide to make sugar and oxygen. They release most of the oxygen into the air. (*See* **breathing** and **photosynthesis.**)

Since oxygen combines easily with many elements, a great deal of it exists in *compounds*—chemically bound elements. Water is a compound of oxygen and hydrogen. Oxygen combined with a metal (such as tin) or a nonmetal (such as silicon) is called an *oxide.* Rust—a compound of oxygen and iron—is a familiar oxide. When nonmetallic oxides combine with hydrogen, they form acids. Oxygen also exists as *free oxygen* —not combined with other elements. (*See* **acids and bases.**)

By itself, oxygen will not burn. But if the temperature is high enough, substances will combine with oxygen and burst into flame. We are used to seeing paper and wood burn, but with enough heat and oxygen, even some metals will burn.

Sometimes, decaying materials such as damp hay or oily rags will generate enough heat to set themselves on fire. This is called *spontaneous combustion,* because the substances seem to catch fire by themselves.

Oxygen high in the atmosphere protects us from the sun's ultraviolet rays. Thirty miles above the earth, the oxygen turns into a poisonous gas called *ozone.* It absorbs many of the cancer-causing rays. Soon it changes back into safe oxygen. (*See* **ultraviolet light.**)

Although oxygen is not a metal, it is slightly magnetic. When it turns into a liquid at $-219°$ C ($-362°$ F), its magnetism increases. At such low temperatures, mixtures of copper oxide and metals called *rare earths* conduct electricity very easily. Scientists call such oxides *supermagnetic* and *superconductive.* They are developing oxides that will remain supermagnetic and superconductive at higher temperatures so that we can have cheaper electricity. (*See* **magnetism.**)

oyster

The oyster is a mollusk that lives in shallow parts of the ocean. Its soft body is protected by a hard shell. The shell has two halves that are hinged on one side. The outside of the shell is rough, sometimes even covered with spines. The inside surface of the shell is smooth and pearly. This shiny substance is called *mother-of-pearl.* (*See* **mollusk.**)

The oyster feeds on bacteria, algae, and other tiny organisms. It opens its shell when it eats. It tightly closes the shell when it is frightened or out of water. It is very difficult to pry an oyster's shell open.

The eastern oyster (top) is good to eat. The great pearl oyster (below) can make a pearl inside its shell.

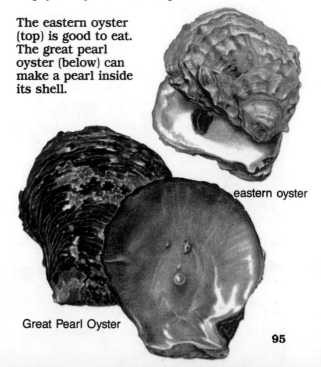

eastern oyster

Great Pearl Oyster

Oyster farmers grow oysters in racks like this one in a saltwater bay.

Oysters hatch from eggs. The baby oysters are as small as the point of a needle and do not have shells. They each have a muscular foot and swim through the water. In a few days, they attach themselves to a rock or other hard underwater object. Gradually, they build thick shells. They stay in that spot for the rest of their lives.

Oysters are important to people. They are a popular food. Sea farmers have found ways to grow crops of oysters in shallow water. Some oysters make pearls, which people use for jewelry. People also use mother-of-pearl to make jewelry and buttons. (*See* **pearl**.)

Ozark Mountains

The Ozark Mountains are a range of low, rugged hills in the south-central United States. They cover parts of Illinois, Missouri, Arkansas, and Oklahoma. The Ozark Mountains are also called the Ozark Plateau or the Ozarks. The Ozarks' highest peaks—the Boston Mountains in Arkansas—are just over 2,000 feet (600 meters).

The name *Ozarks* comes from the French words *aux Arks*. It means "at the Arks"— that is, at the land of the Arkansas Indians, who once lived in the area.

The Ozarks have great natural beauty. Thick forests cover the hills. Swift, sparkling streams make their way through hollows and along valley floors. Natural springs and caves are plentiful.

In the past, not many people lived in the Ozarks. Those who did were farmers, growing fruits, corn, and wheat. Today, it is a fast-growing area. Many older people have retired there to live in beautiful surroundings. Rivers have been dammed to make lakes for vacationers. Industry has moved there, too.

Two areas have been set aside to preserve the natural beauty of the Ozarks. One is the Ozark National Forest in Arkansas. The other is the Ozark National Scenic Riverways, along the Current River in Missouri.

A wood cabin nestles among the trees in the gently rolling Ozark Mountains.